SURVIVAL OF THE FITTEST

6 FIERCE ANIMAL COMPETITORS

3 SHARK JUDGES

1 WINNER

FOR MY MIDDLE SCHOOL
SCIENCE TEACHERS —M. S.

FOR PHILIP,
ALWAYS A FAIR COMPETITOR —R. D.

HENRY HOLT AND COMPANY, *PUBLISHERS SINCE 1866*
HENRY HOLT® IS A REGISTERED TRADEMARK OF MACMILLAN PUBLISHING GROUP, LLC
120 BROADWAY, NEW YORK, NY 10271 • MACKIDS.COM

OUR BOOKS MAY BE PURCHASED IN BULK FOR PROMOTIONAL, EDUCATIONAL, OR BUSINESS USE.
PLEASE CONTACT YOUR LOCAL BOOKSELLER OR THE MACMILLAN CORPORATE AND PREMIUM SALES DEPARTMENT AT (800)
221-7945 EXT. 5442 OR BY EMAIL AT MACMILLANSPECIALMARKETS@MACMILLAN.COM.

LIBRARY OF CONGRESS CONTROL NUMBER: 2023937822

FIRST EDITION, 2024
BOOK DESIGN BY JESSICA RODRIGUEZ
THE ART FOR THIS BOOK WAS CREATED IN CLIP STUDIO PAINT AND PHOTOSHOP.
PRINTED IN CHINA BY RR DONNELLEY ASIA PRINTING SOLUTIONS LTD., DONGGUAN CITY, GUANGDONG PROVINCE

ISBN 978-1-250-80531-7
1 3 5 7 9 10 8 6 4 2

SURVIVAL ⚙ OF THE ⚙ FITTEST

6 FIERCE ANIMAL COMPETITORS
3 SHARK JUDGES
1 WINNER

WHO
WILL COME
OUT ON TOP?

Written by
REBECCA DONNELLY

Illustrated by
MISA SABURI

HENRY HOLT AND COMPANY
NEW YORK

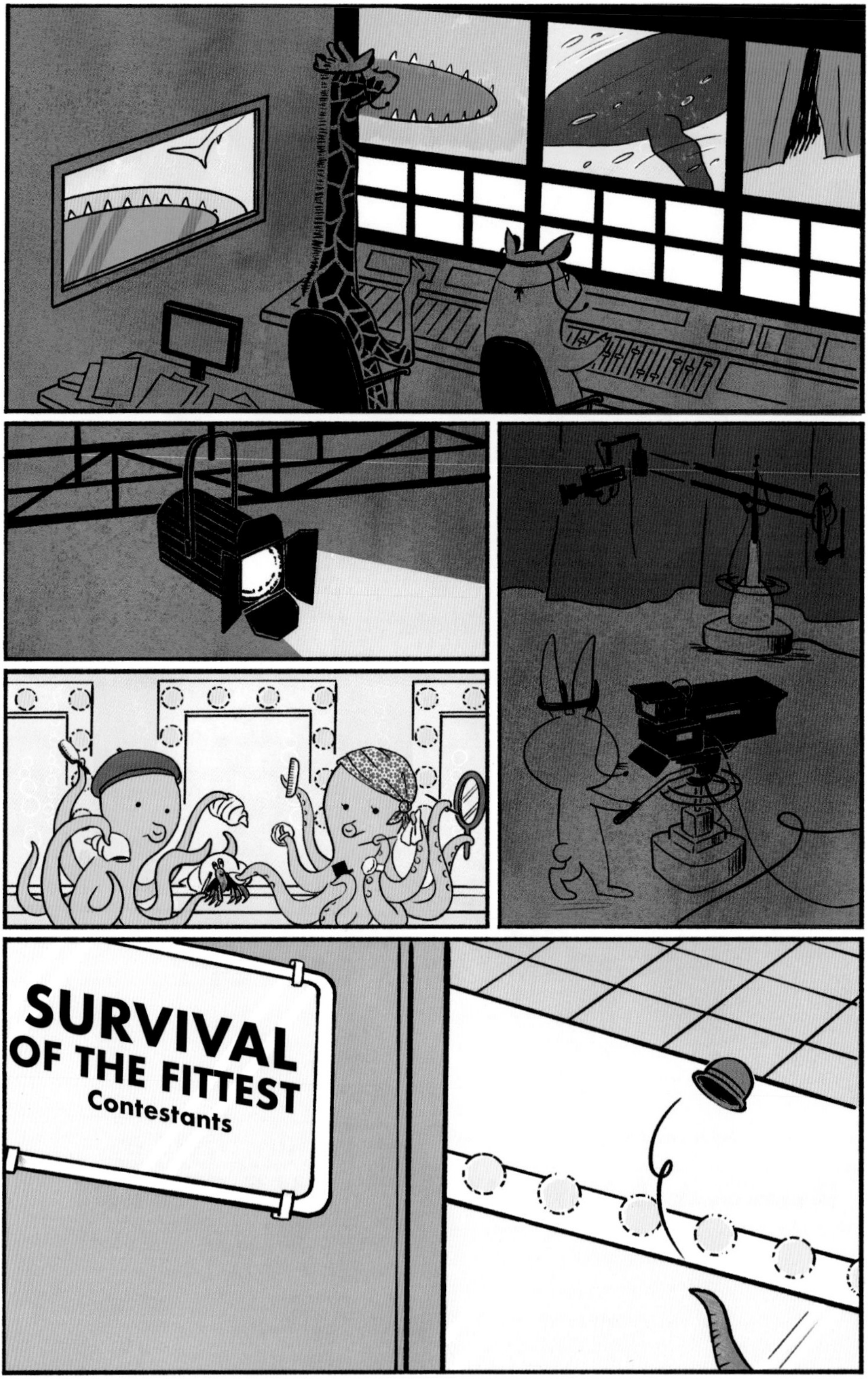
SURVIVAL
OF THE FITTEST
Contestants

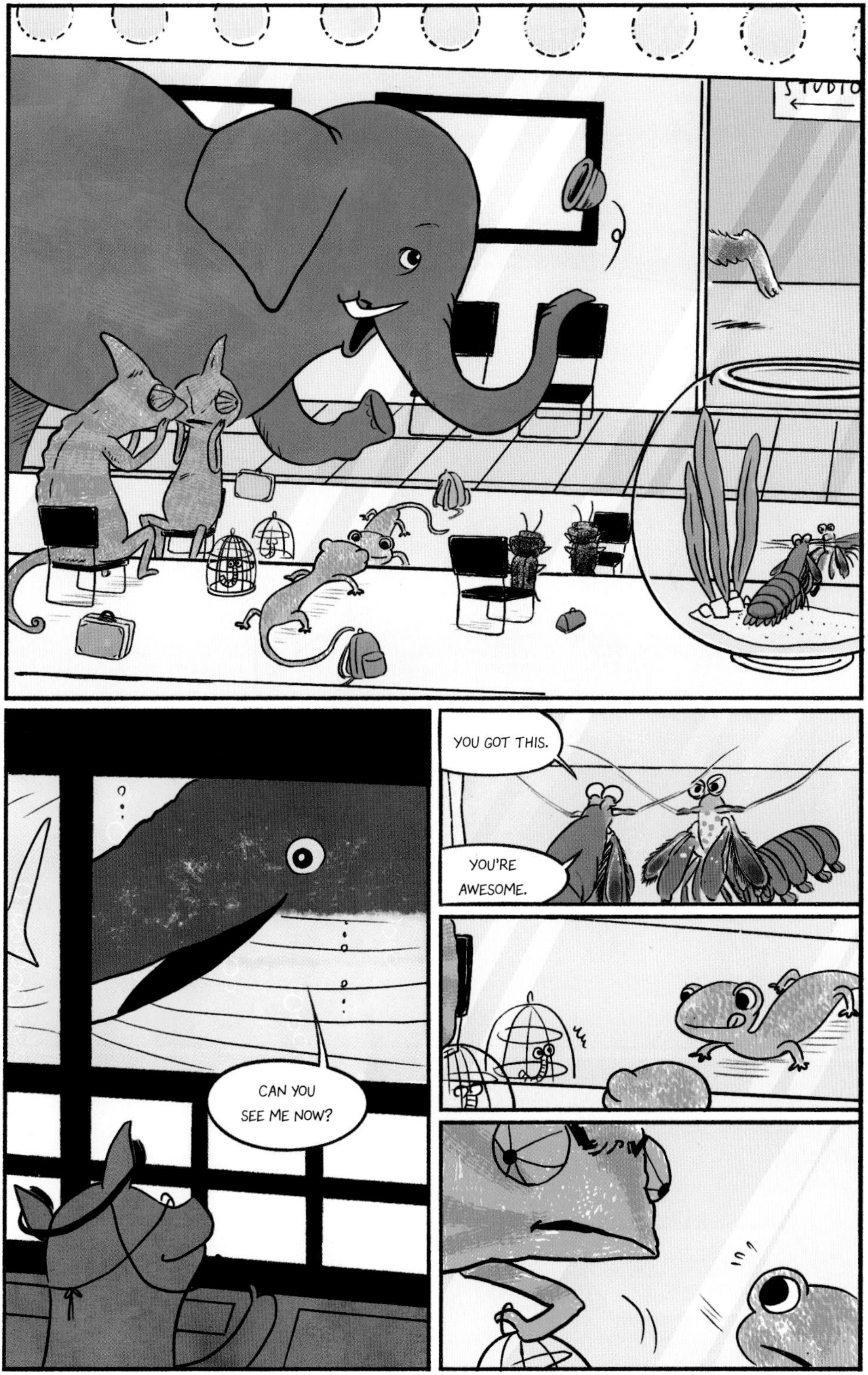
STUDIO
CAN YOU SEE ME NOW?
YOU GOT THIS.
YOU'RE AWESOME.

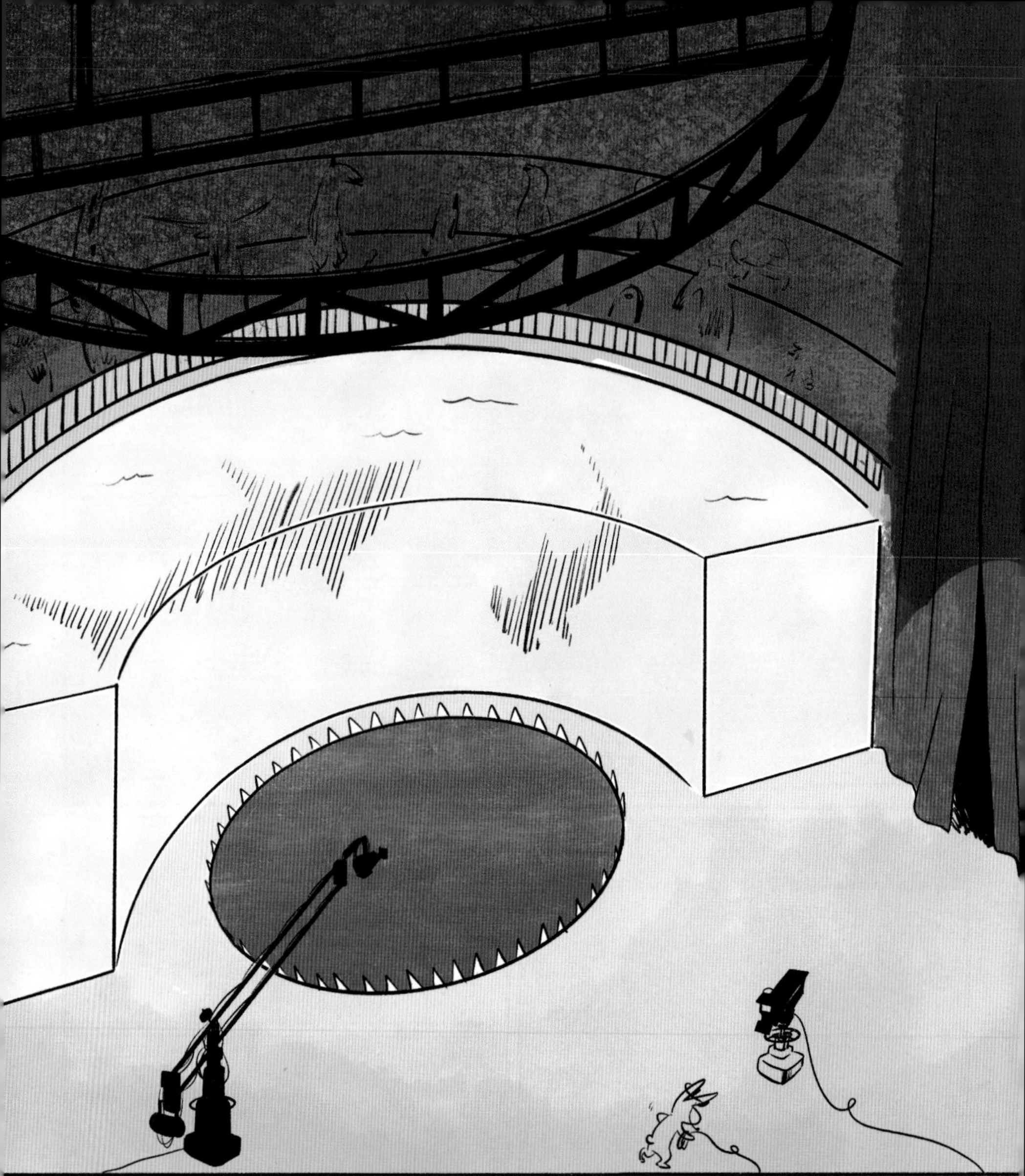

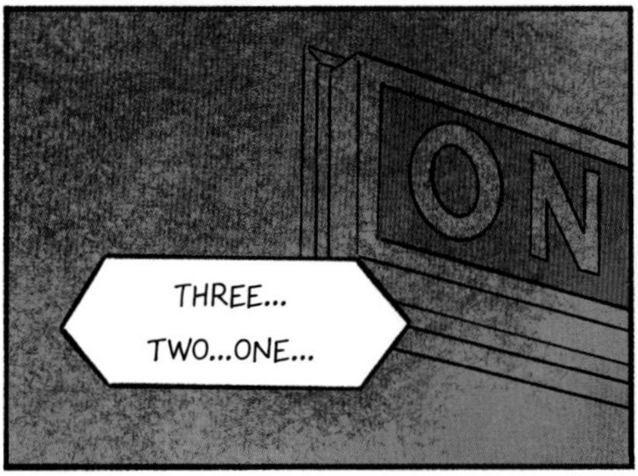
ON
THREE...
TWO...ONE...

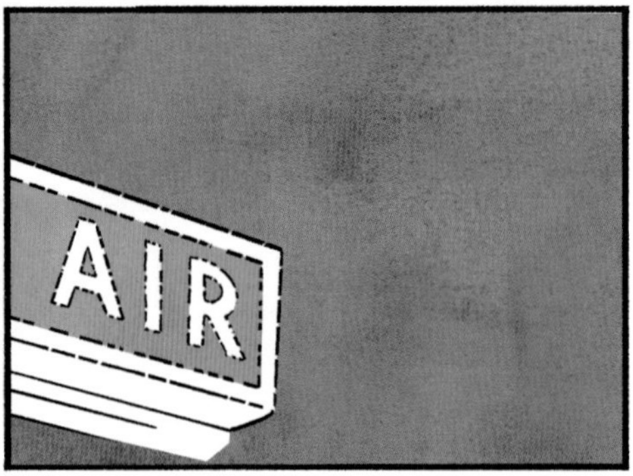
AIR

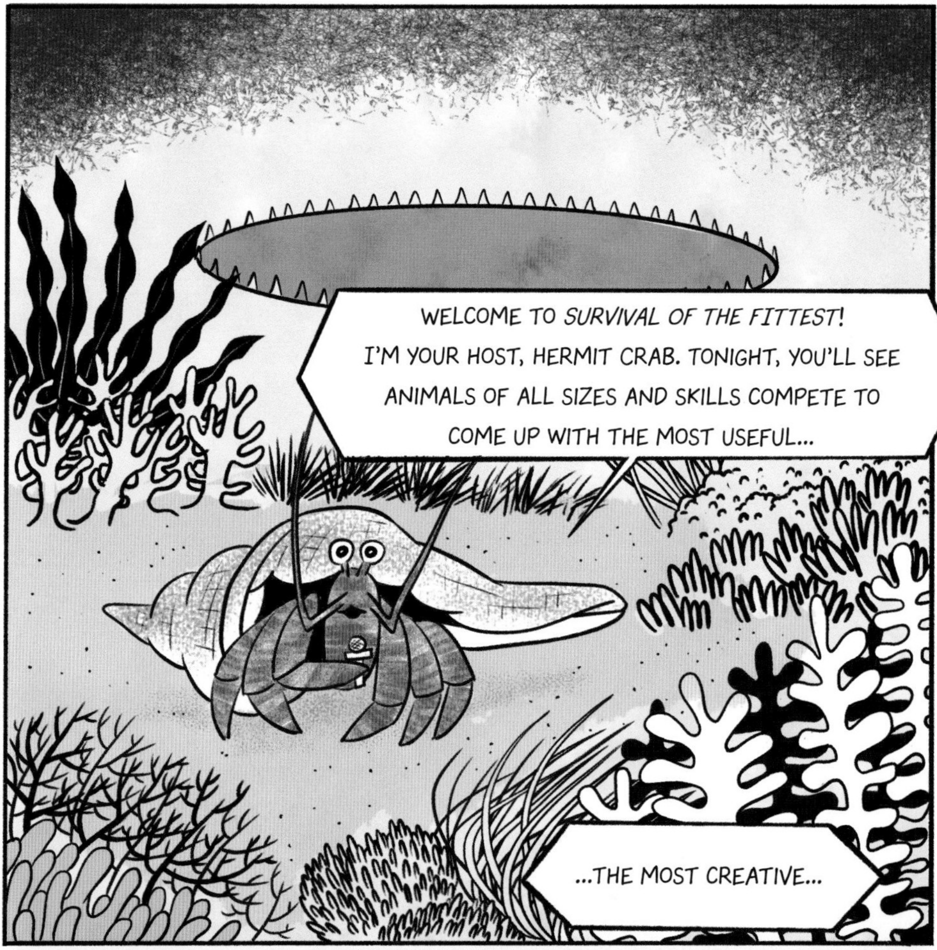
WELCOME TO *SURVIVAL OF THE FITTEST*! I'M YOUR HOST, HERMIT CRAB. TONIGHT, YOU'LL SEE ANIMALS OF ALL SIZES AND SKILLS COMPETE TO COME UP WITH THE MOST USEFUL...
...THE MOST CREATIVE...

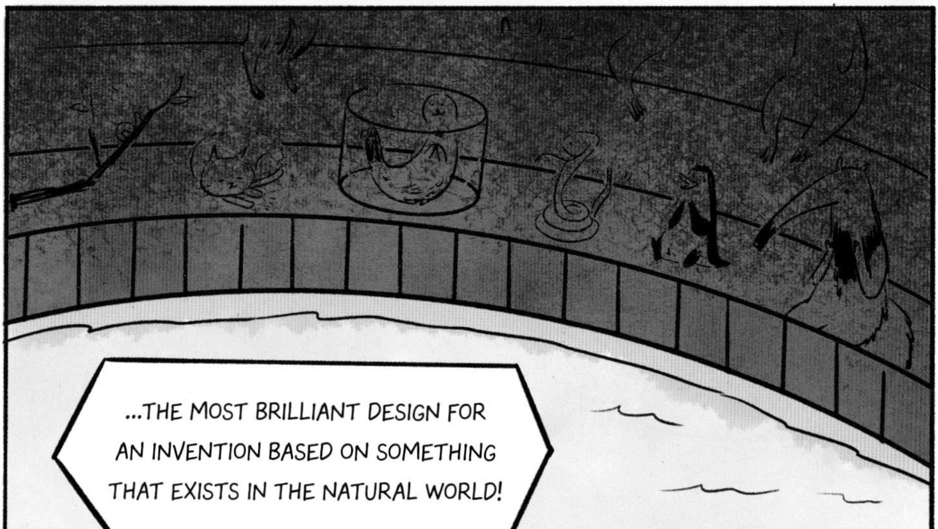
...THE MOST BRILLIANT DESIGN FOR AN INVENTION BASED ON SOMETHING THAT EXISTS IN THE NATURAL WORLD!

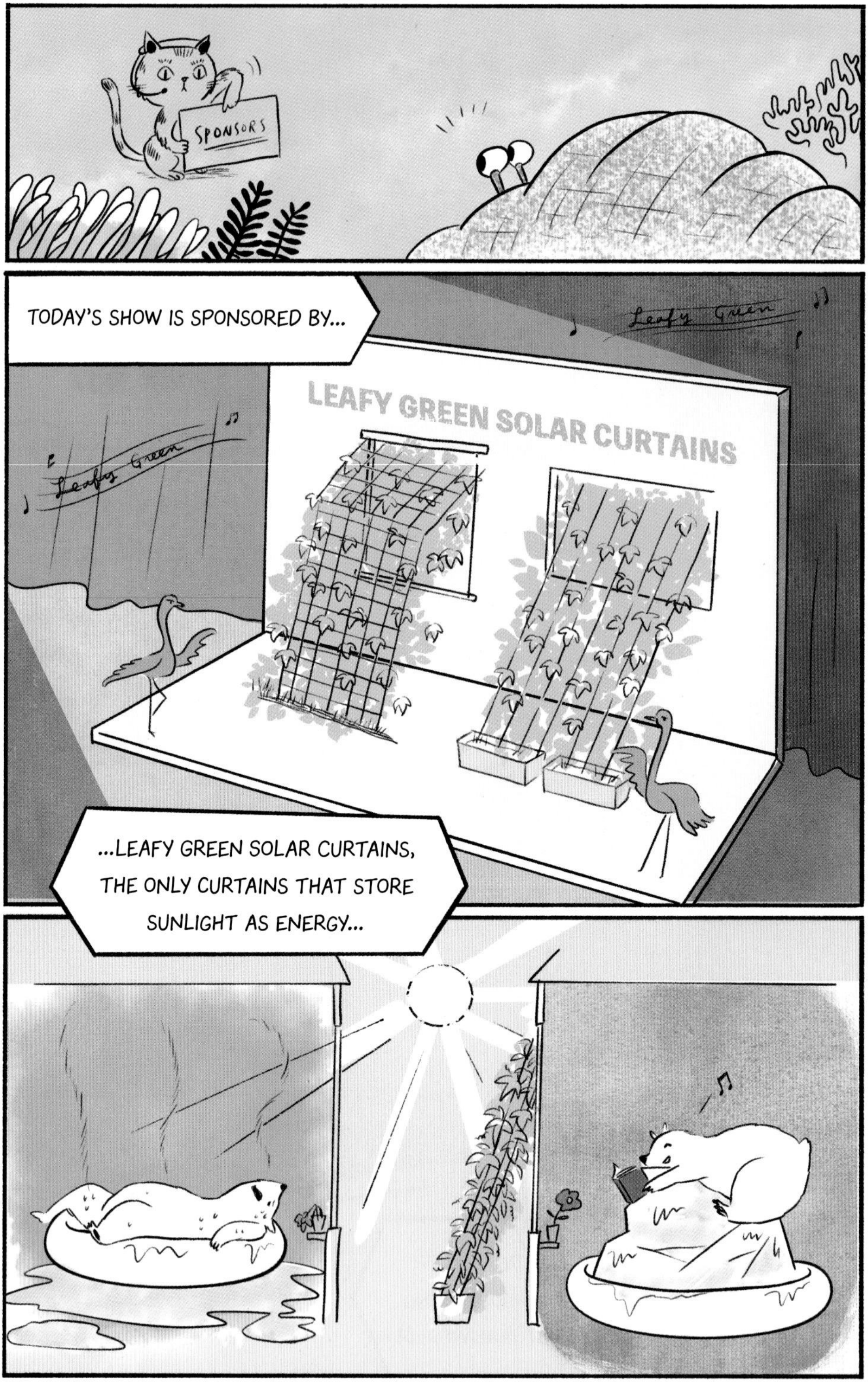
SPONSORS
TODAY'S SHOW IS SPONSORED BY...
Leafy Green
LEAFY GREEN SOLAR CURTAINS
Leafy Green
...LEAFY GREEN SOLAR CURTAINS, THE ONLY CURTAINS THAT STORE SUNLIGHT AS ENERGY...

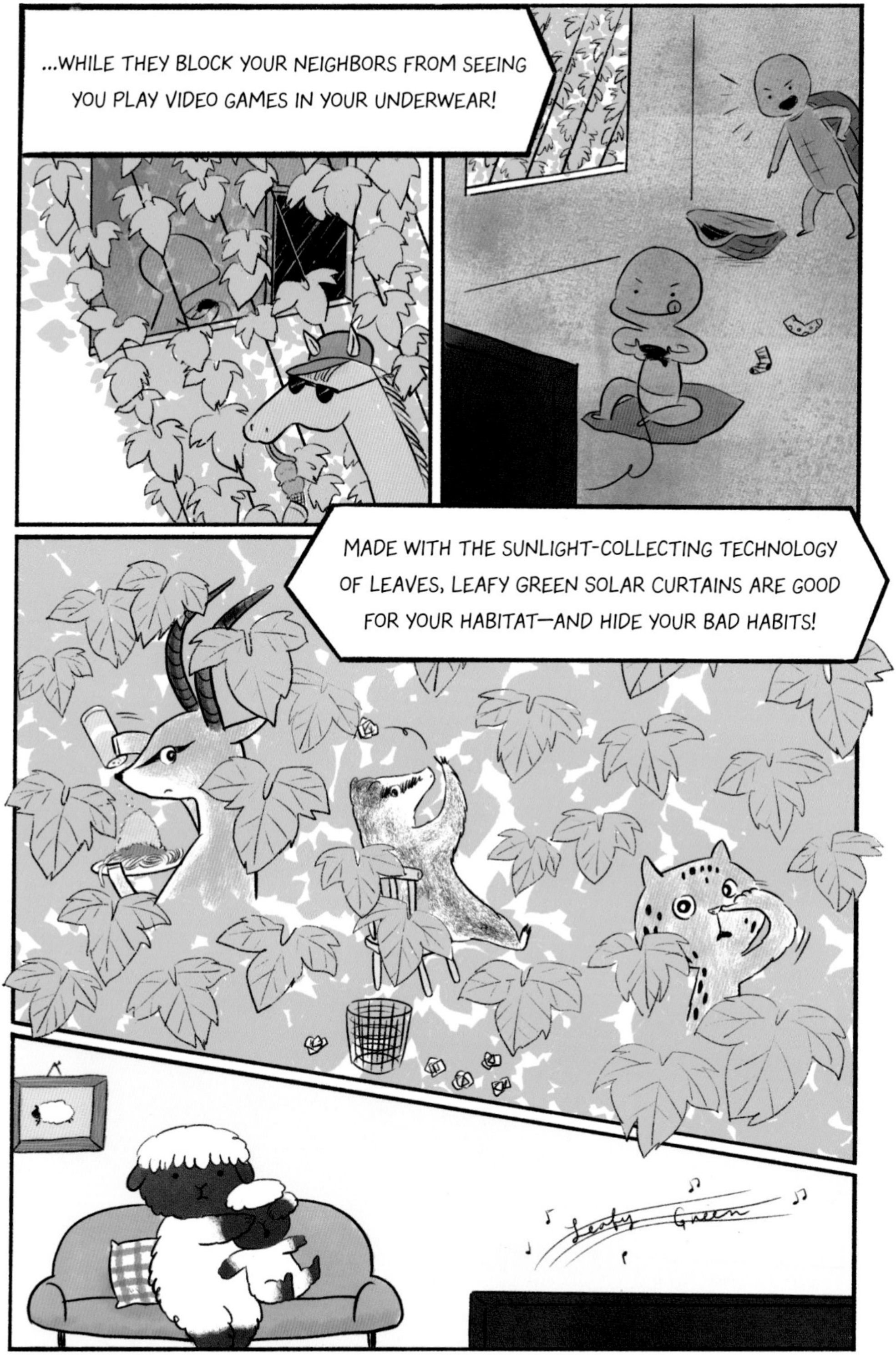
...WHILE THEY BLOCK YOUR NEIGHBORS FROM SEEING YOU PLAY VIDEO GAMES IN YOUR UNDERWEAR!
MADE WITH THE SUNLIGHT-COLLECTING TECHNOLOGY OF LEAVES, LEAFY GREEN SOLAR CURTAINS ARE GOOD FOR YOUR HABITAT—AND HIDE YOUR BAD HABITS!
Leafy Green

CHAPTER
ONE

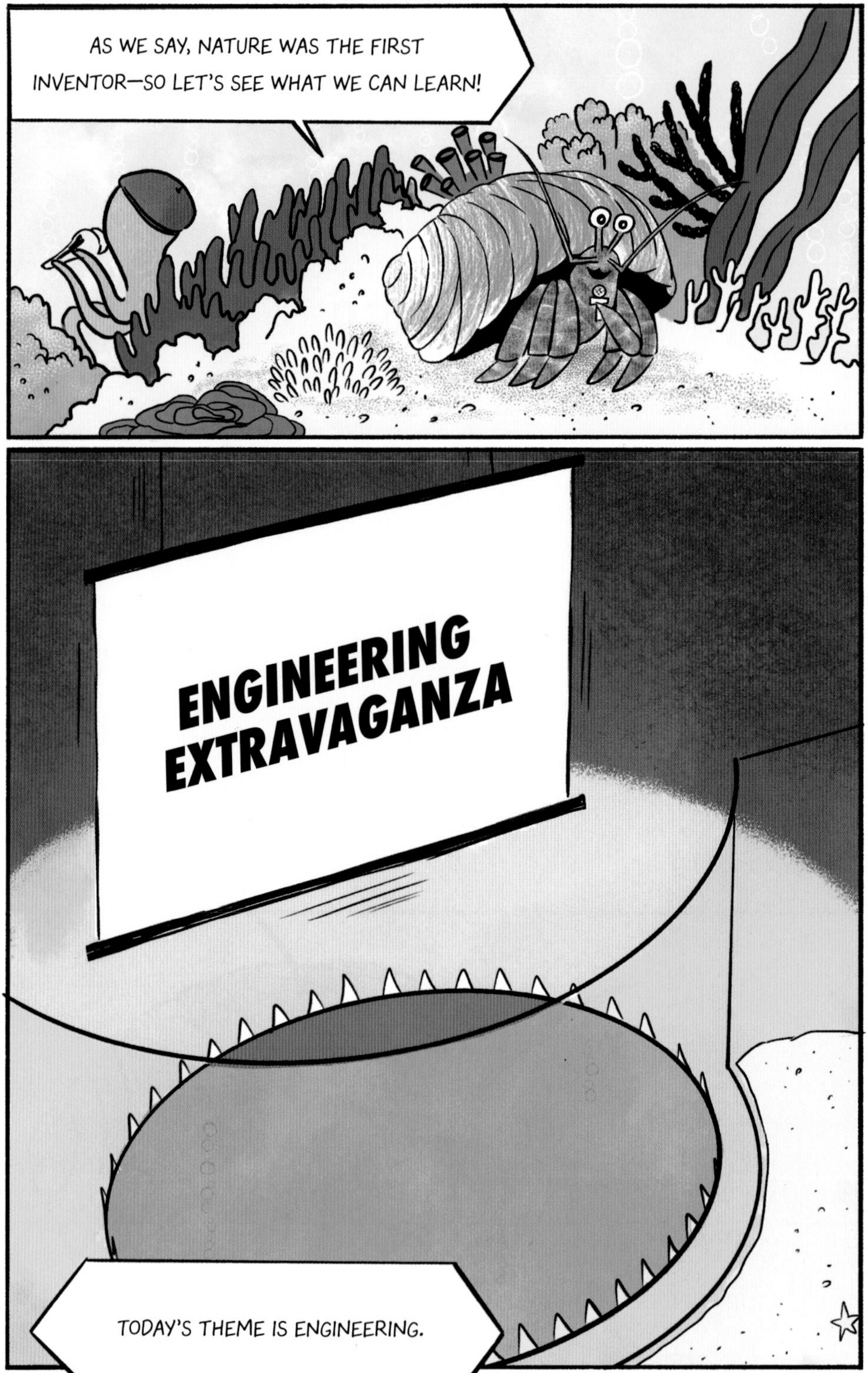
AS WE SAY, NATURE WAS THE FIRST INVENTOR—SO LET'S SEE WHAT WE CAN LEARN!
ENGINEERING EXTRAVAGANZA
TODAY'S THEME IS ENGINEERING.

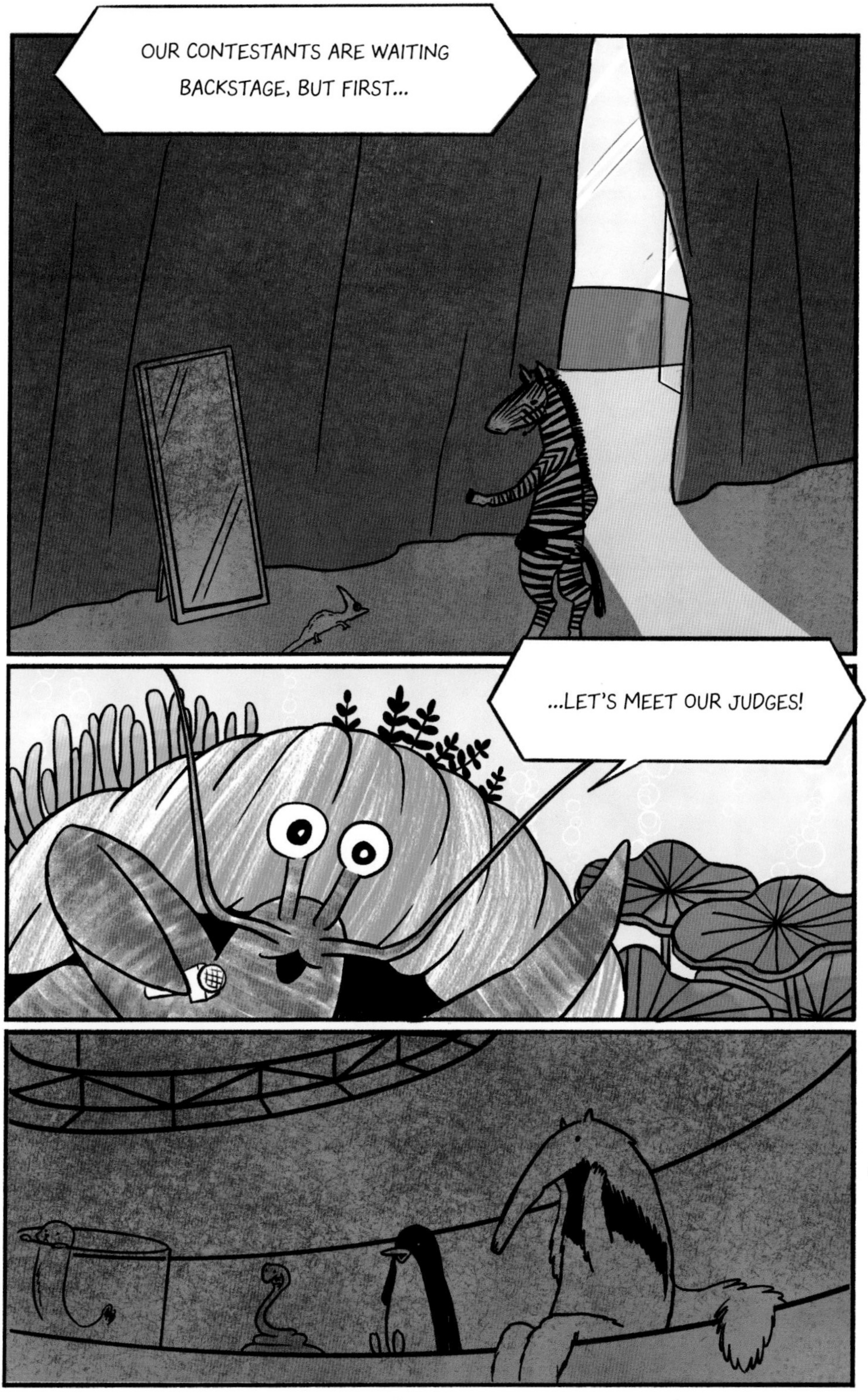
OUR CONTESTANTS ARE WAITING BACKSTAGE, BUT FIRST...
...LET'S MEET OUR JUDGES!

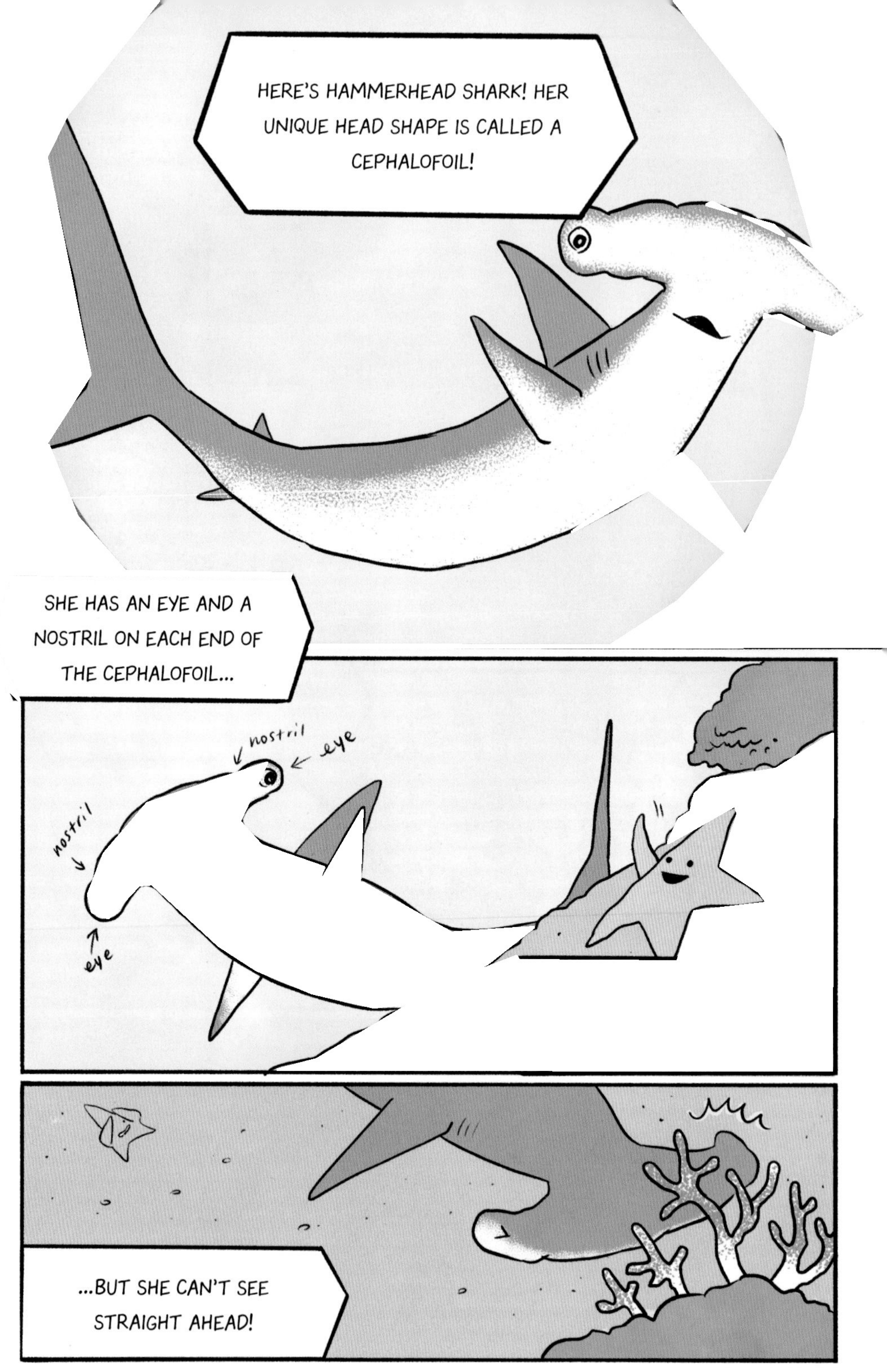
HERE'S HAMMERHEAD SHARK! HER UNIQUE HEAD SHAPE IS CALLED A CEPHALOFOIL!
SHE HAS AN EYE AND A NOSTRIL ON EACH END OF THE CEPHALOFOIL...
nostril
eye
nostril
eye
...BUT SHE CAN'T SEE STRAIGHT AHEAD!

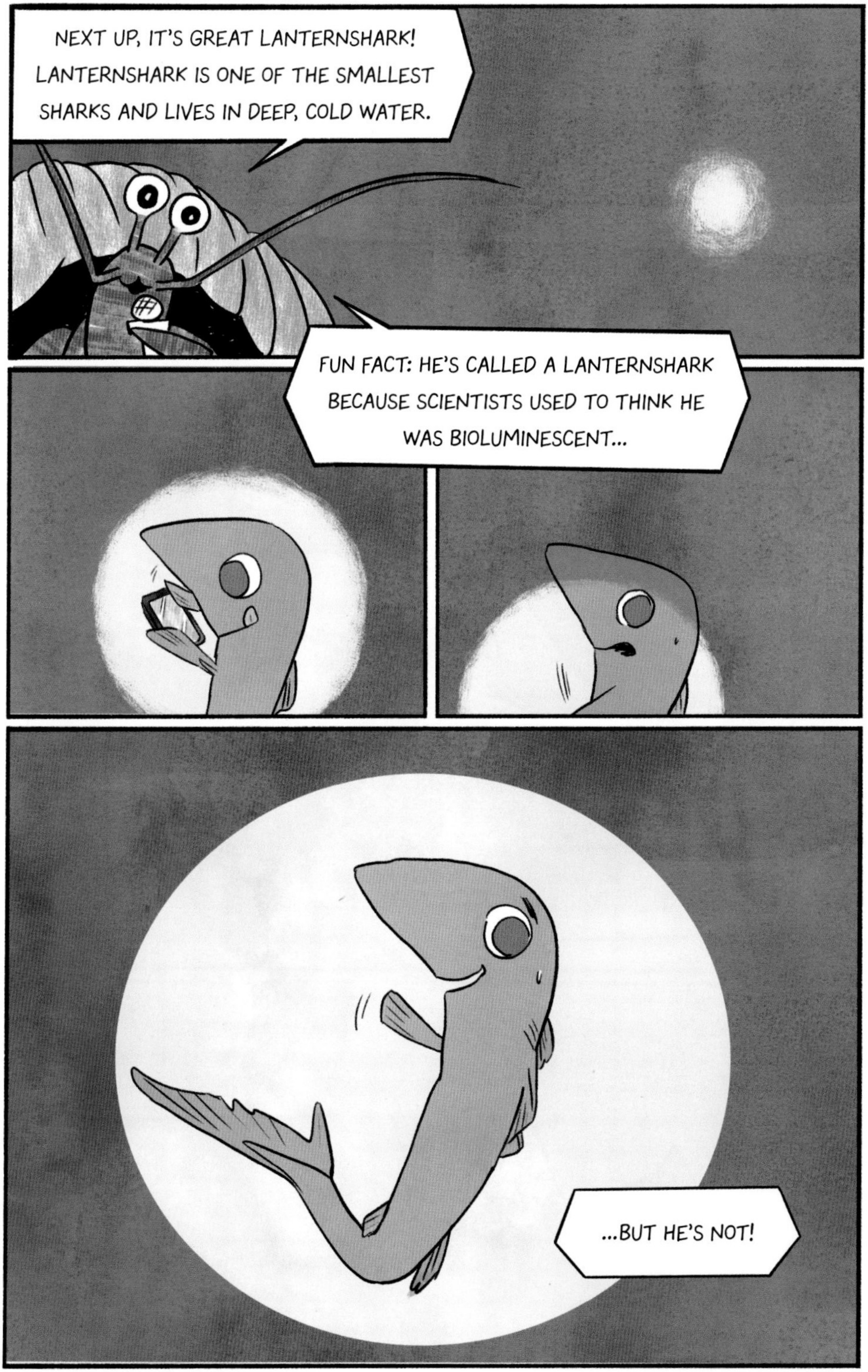
NEXT UP, IT'S GREAT LANTERNSHARK! LANTERNSHARK IS ONE OF THE SMALLEST SHARKS AND LIVES IN DEEP, COLD WATER.
FUN FACT: HE'S CALLED A LANTERNSHARK BECAUSE SCIENTISTS USED TO THINK HE WAS BIOLUMINESCENT...
...BUT HE'S NOT!

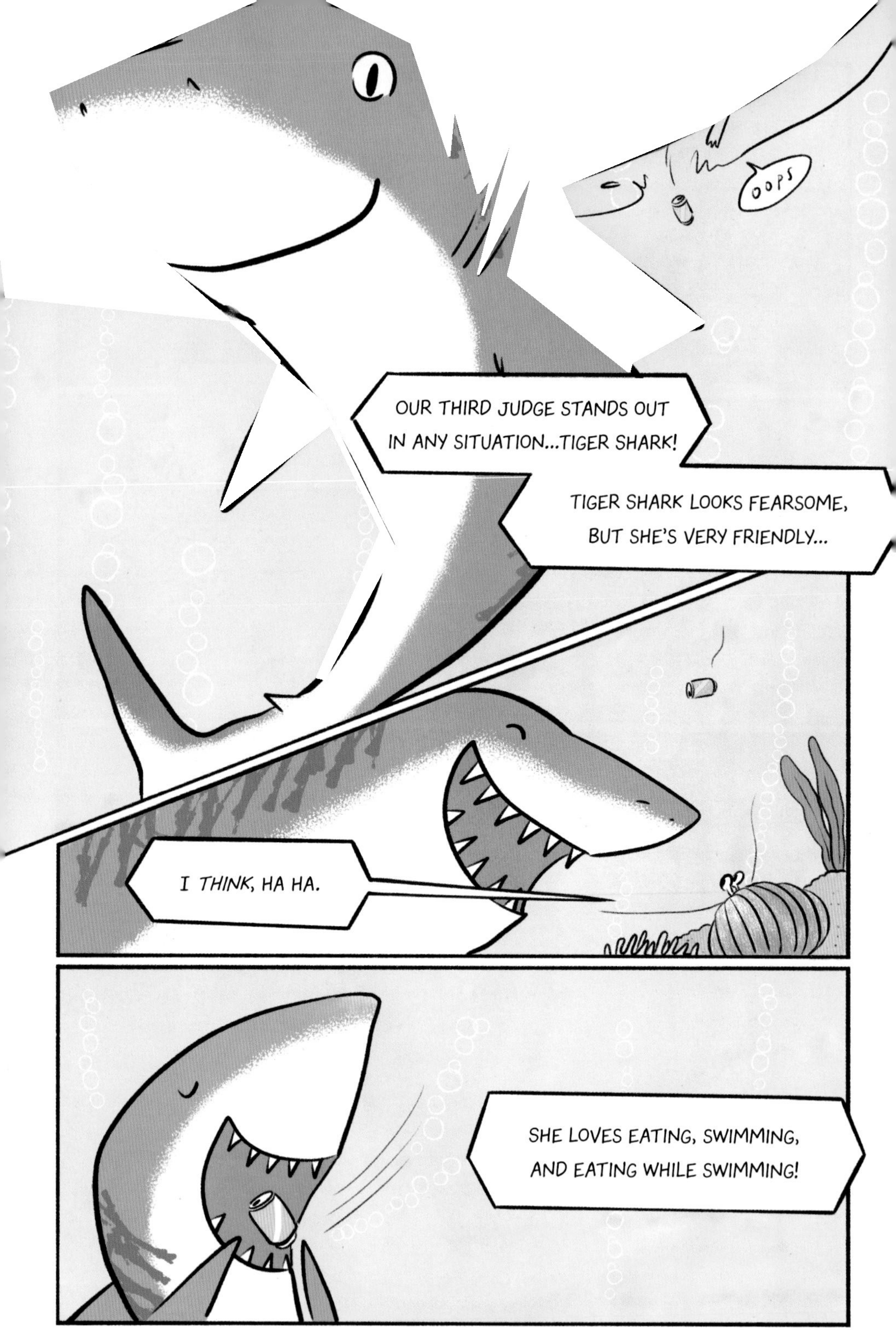
OOPS
OUR THIRD JUDGE STANDS OUT IN ANY SITUATION...TIGER SHARK!
TIGER SHARK LOOKS FEARSOME, BUT SHE'S VERY FRIENDLY...
I THINK, HA HA.
SHE LOVES EATING, SWIMMING, AND EATING WHILE SWIMMING!

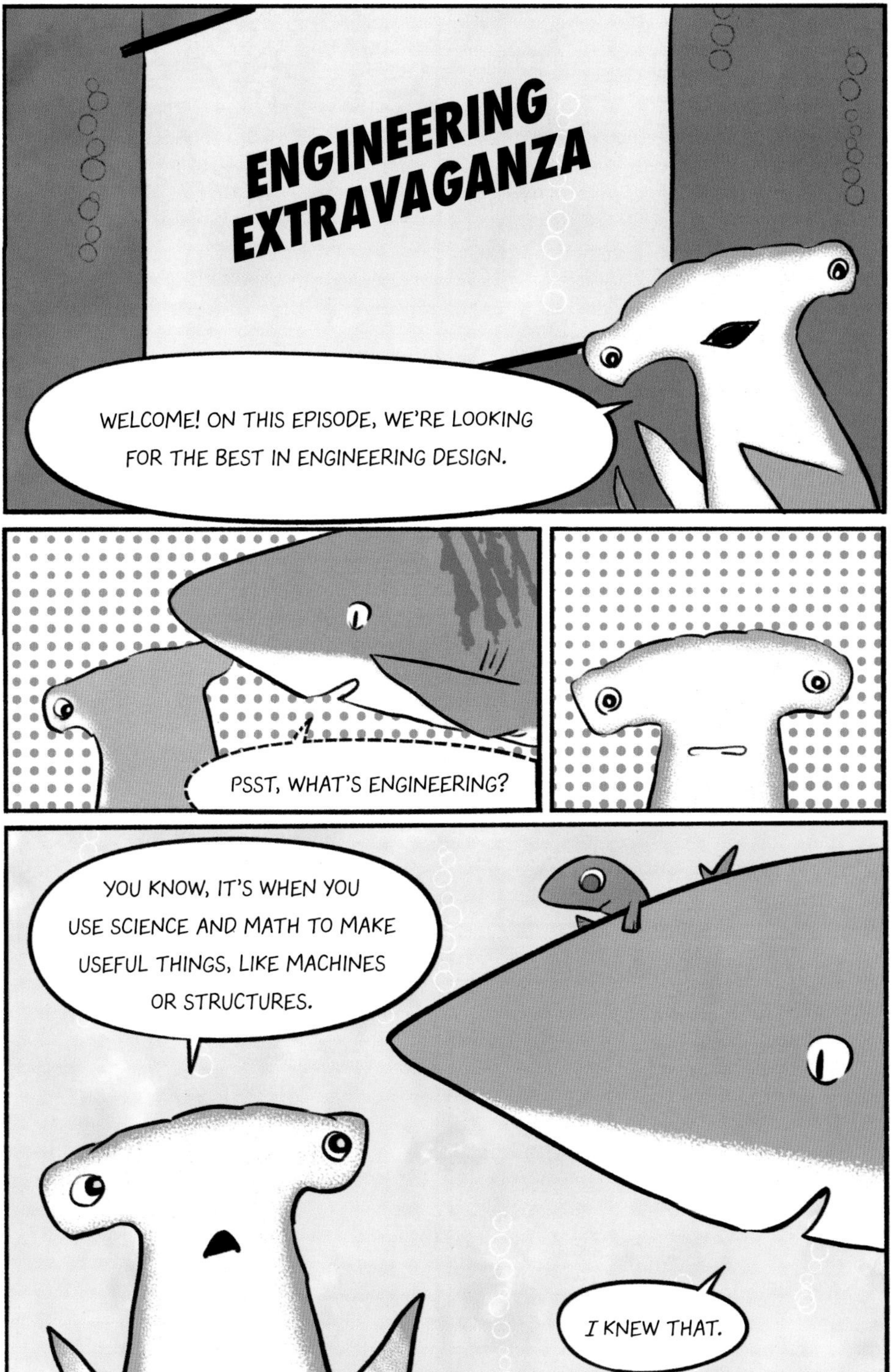
ENGINEERING EXTRAVAGANZA
WELCOME! ON THIS EPISODE, WE'RE LOOKING FOR THE BEST IN ENGINEERING DESIGN.
PSST, WHAT'S ENGINEERING?
YOU KNOW, IT'S WHEN YOU USE SCIENCE AND MATH TO MAKE USEFUL THINGS, LIKE MACHINES OR STRUCTURES.
I KNEW THAT.

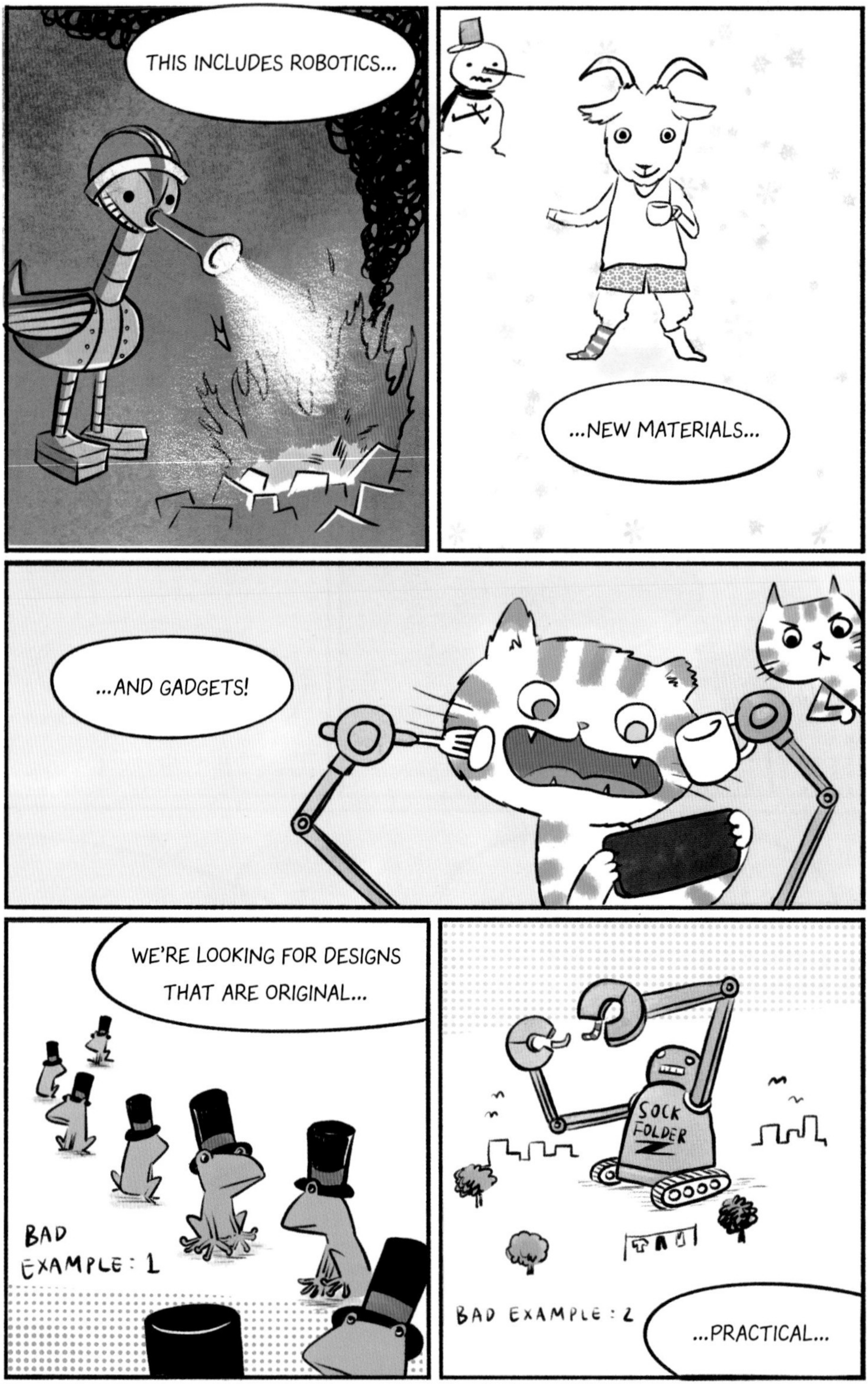
THIS INCLUDES ROBOTICS...
...NEW MATERIALS...
...AND GADGETS!
WE'RE LOOKING FOR DESIGNS THAT ARE ORIGINAL...
BAD EXAMPLE: 1
SOCK FOLDER
BAD EXAMPLE: 2
...PRACTICAL...

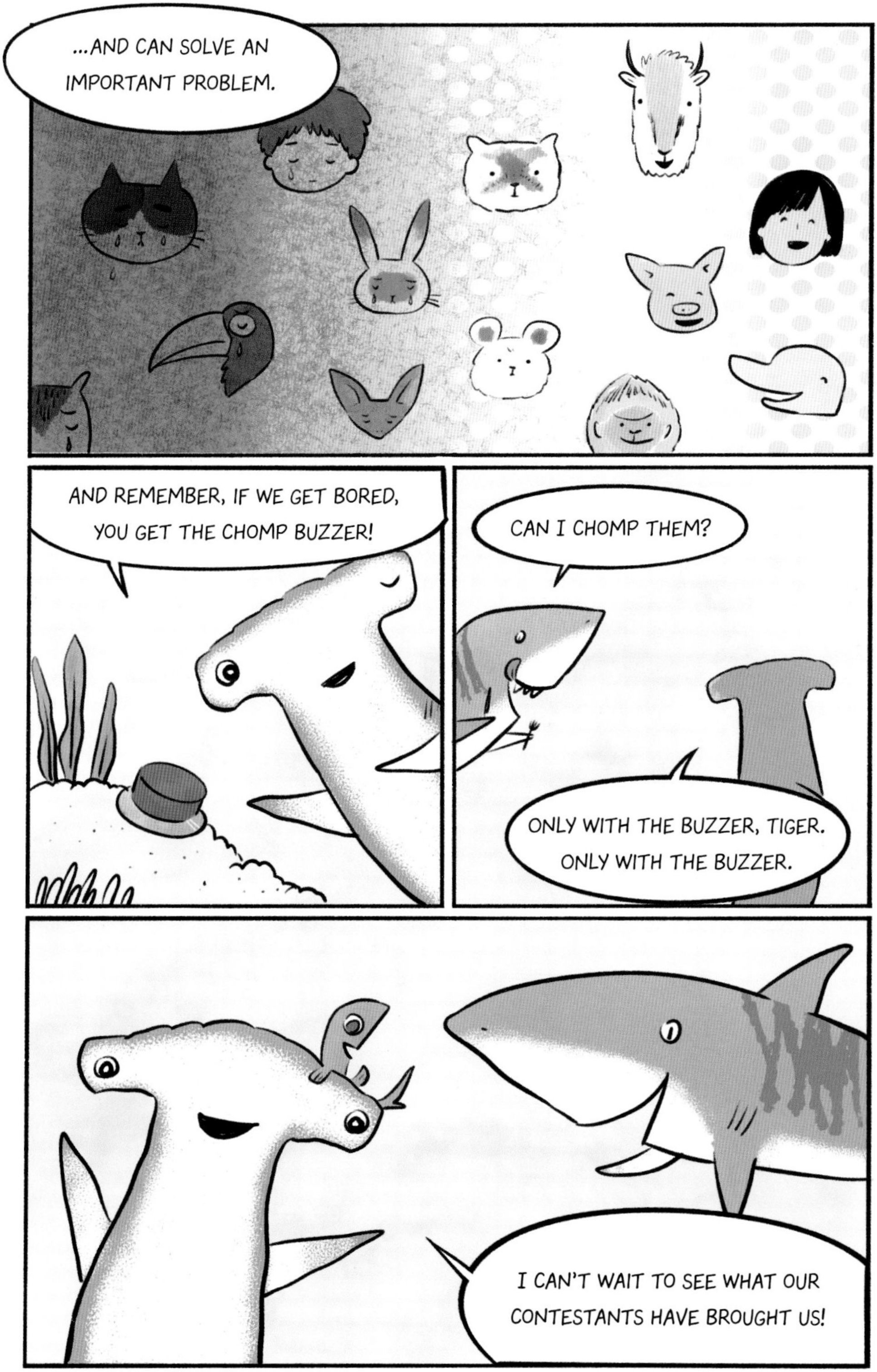
...AND CAN SOLVE AN IMPORTANT PROBLEM.
AND REMEMBER, IF WE GET BORED, YOU GET THE CHOMP BUZZER!
CAN I CHOMP THEM?
ONLY WITH THE BUZZER, TIGER. ONLY WITH THE BUZZER.
I CAN'T WAIT TO SEE WHAT OUR CONTESTANTS HAVE BROUGHT US!

CHAPTER
TWO

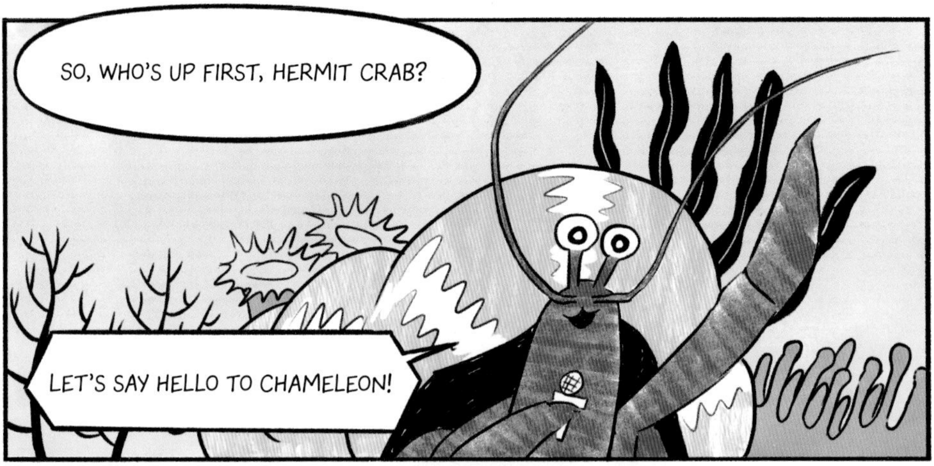
SO, WHO'S UP FIRST, HERMIT CRAB?
LET'S SAY HELLO TO CHAMELEON!

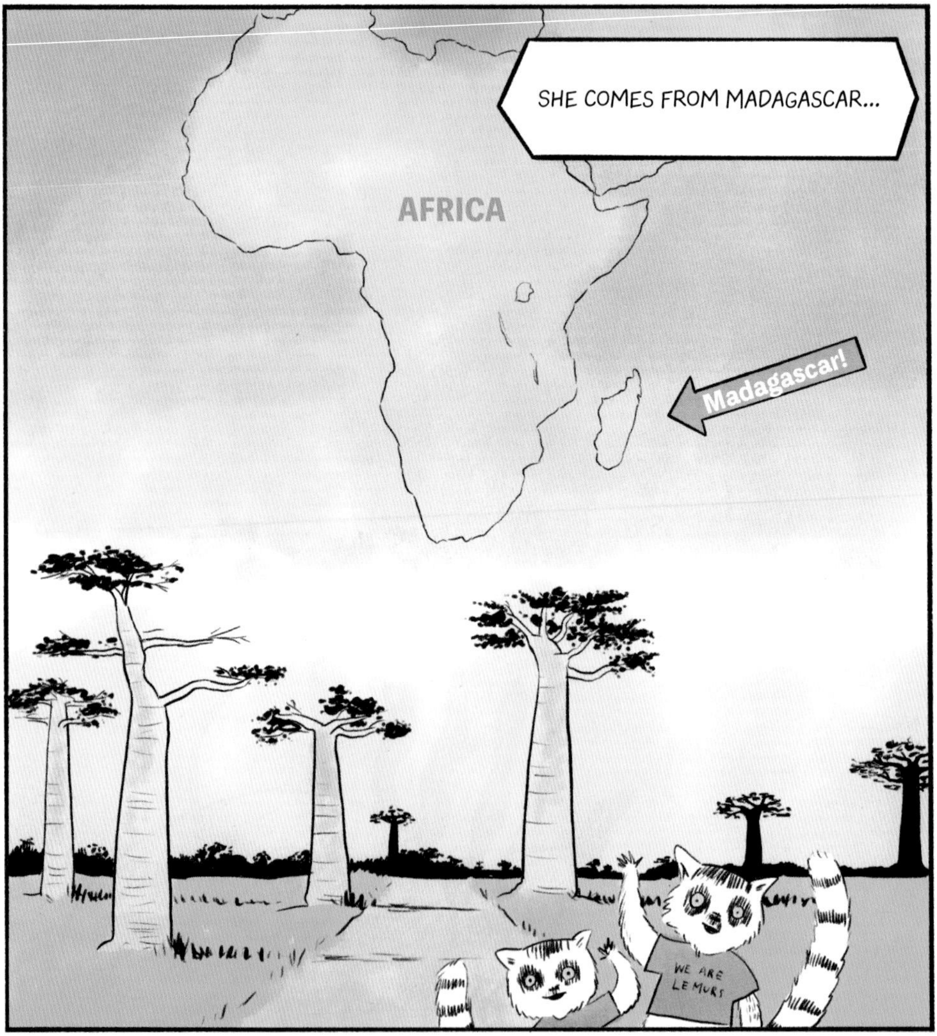
SHE COMES FROM MADAGASCAR...
AFRICA
Madagascar!
WE ARE LEMURS

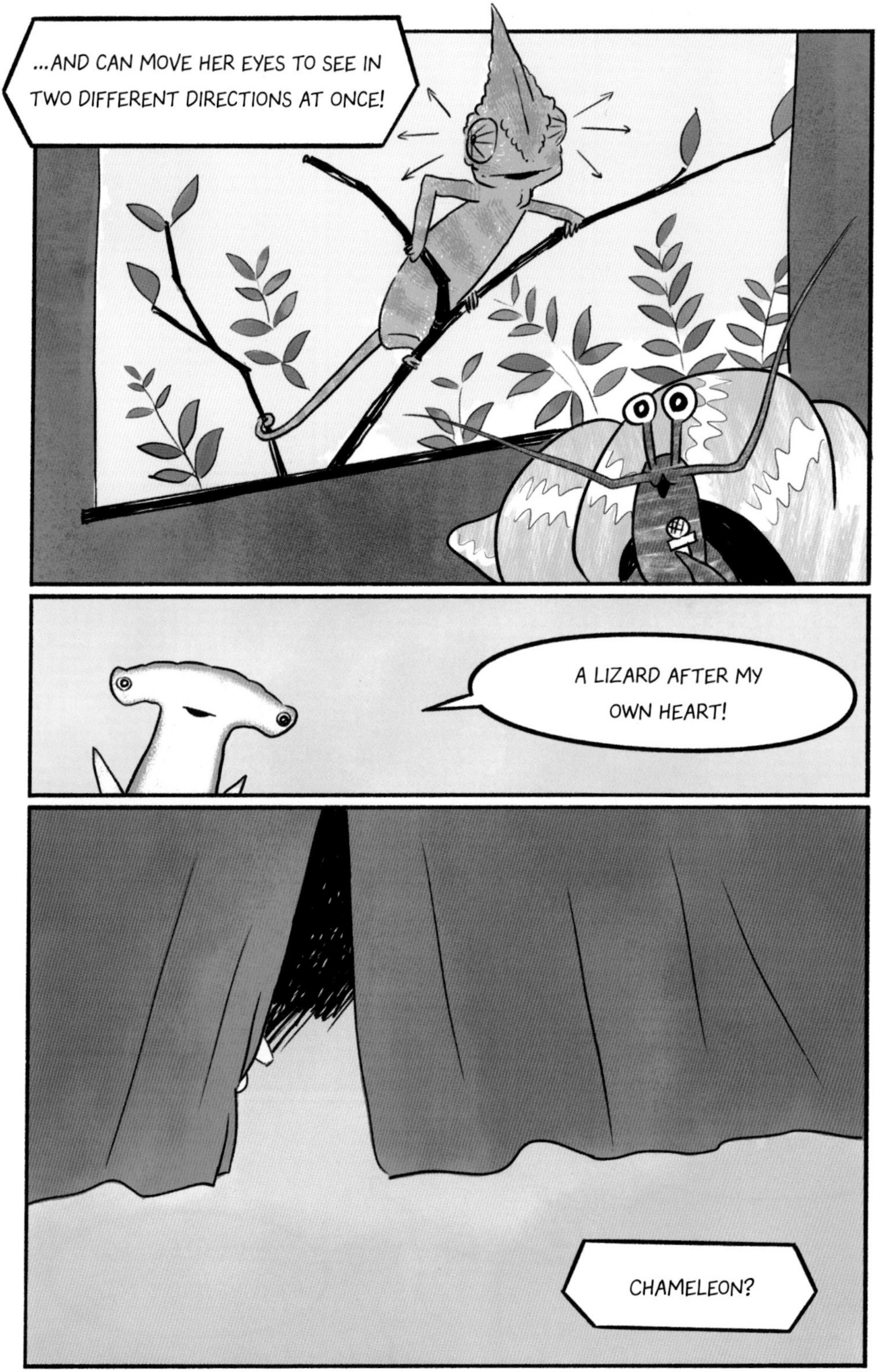
...AND CAN MOVE HER EYES TO SEE IN TWO DIFFERENT DIRECTIONS AT ONCE!
A LIZARD AFTER MY OWN HEART!
CHAMELEON?

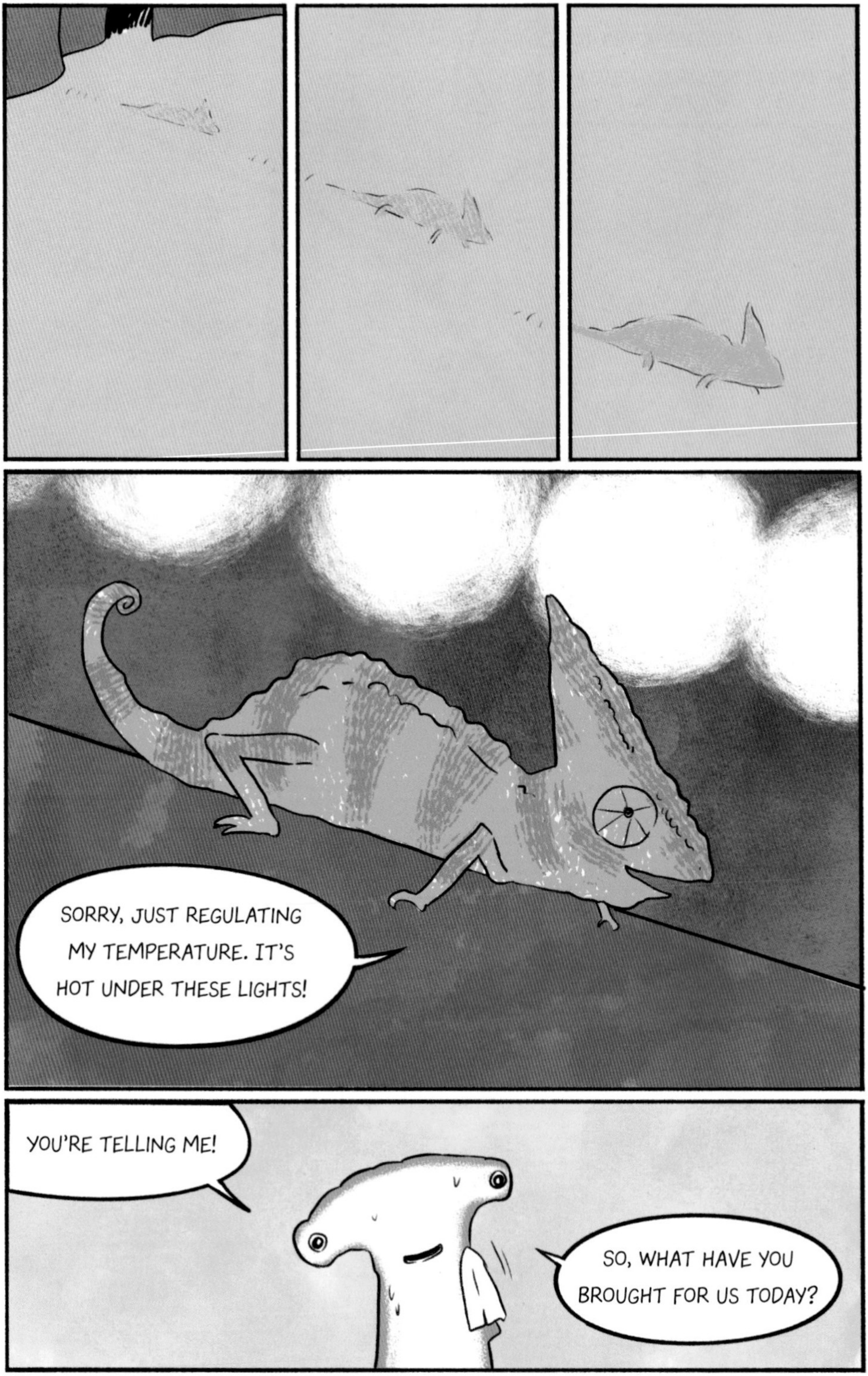
SORRY, JUST REGULATING MY TEMPERATURE. IT'S HOT UNDER THESE LIGHTS!
YOU'RE TELLING ME!
SO, WHAT HAVE YOU BROUGHT FOR US TODAY?

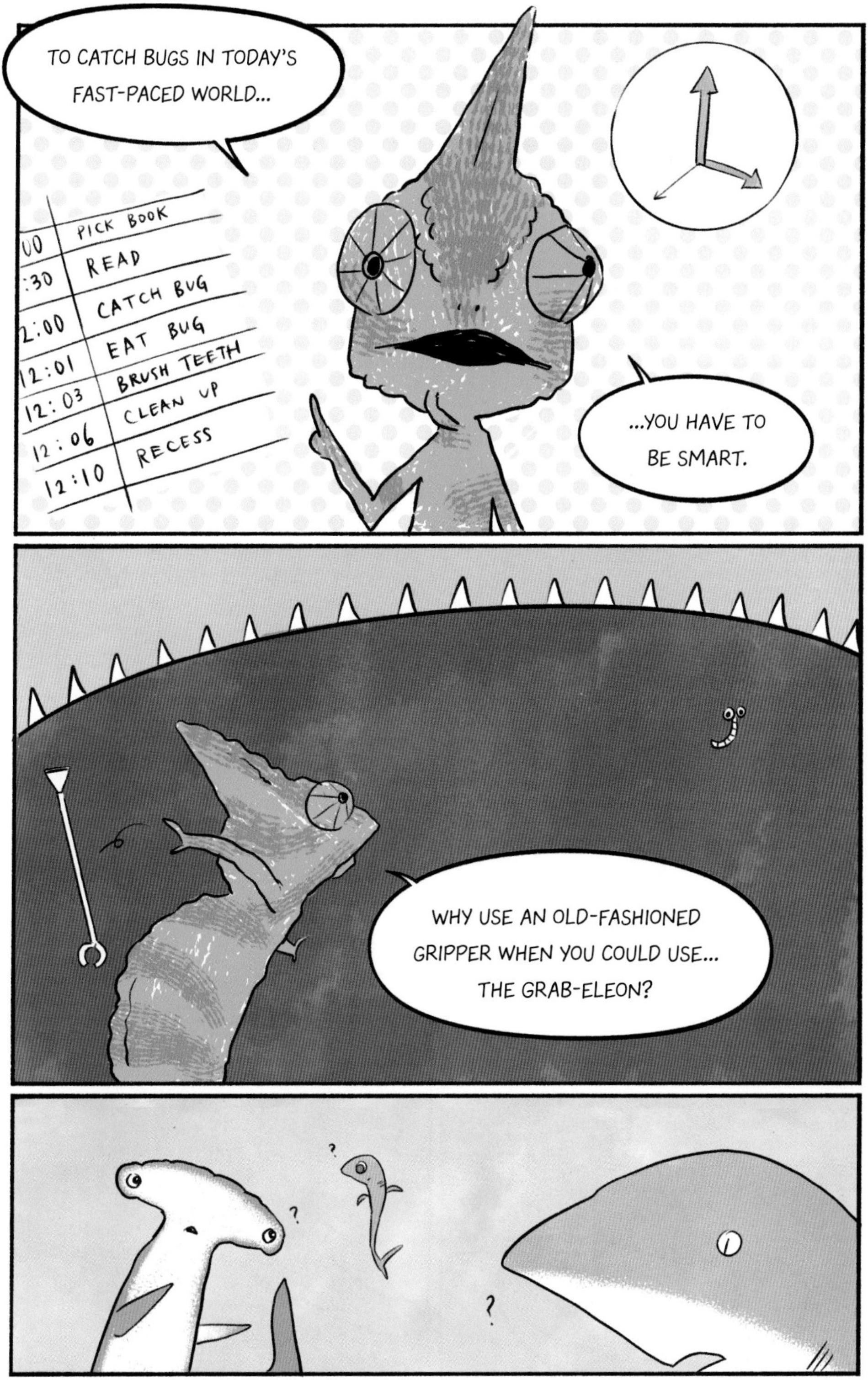
TO CATCH BUGS IN TODAY'S FAST-PACED WORLD...
PICK BOOK
READ
CATCH BUG
EAT BUG
BRUSH TEETH
CLEAN UP
RECESS
00
:30
2:00
12:01
12:03
12:06
12:10
...YOU HAVE TO BE SMART.
WHY USE AN OLD-FASHIONED GRIPPER WHEN YOU COULD USE... THE GRAB-ELEON?

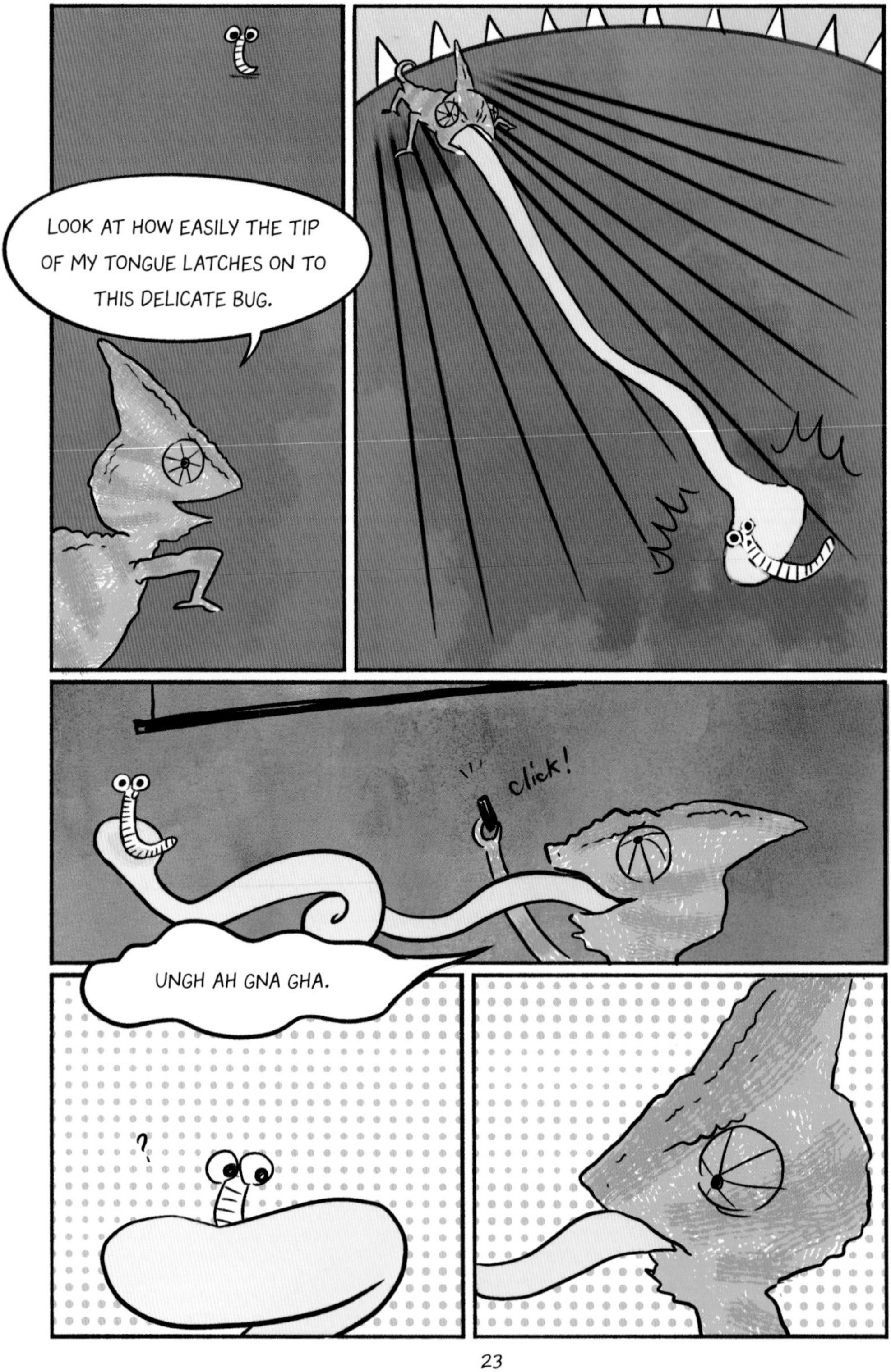
LOOK AT HOW EASILY THE TIP OF MY TONGUE LATCHES ON TO THIS DELICATE BUG.
click!
UNGH AH GNA GHA.
?

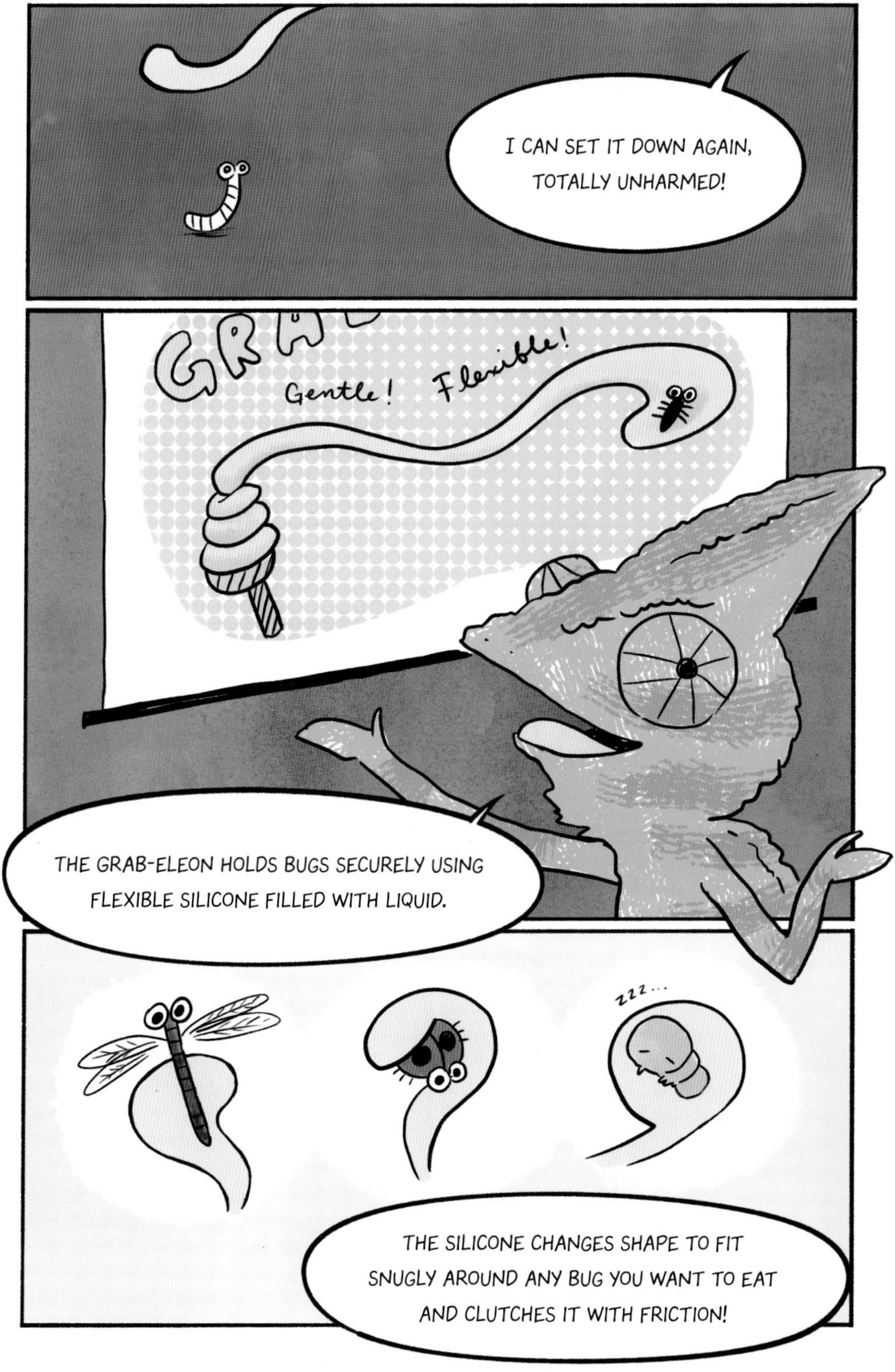
I CAN SET IT DOWN AGAIN, TOTALLY UNHARMED!
GRA
Gentle! Flexible!
THE GRAB-ELEON HOLDS BUGS SECURELY USING FLEXIBLE SILICONE FILLED WITH LIQUID.
zzz...
THE SILICONE CHANGES SHAPE TO FIT SNUGLY AROUND ANY BUG YOU WANT TO EAT AND CLUTCHES IT WITH FRICTION!

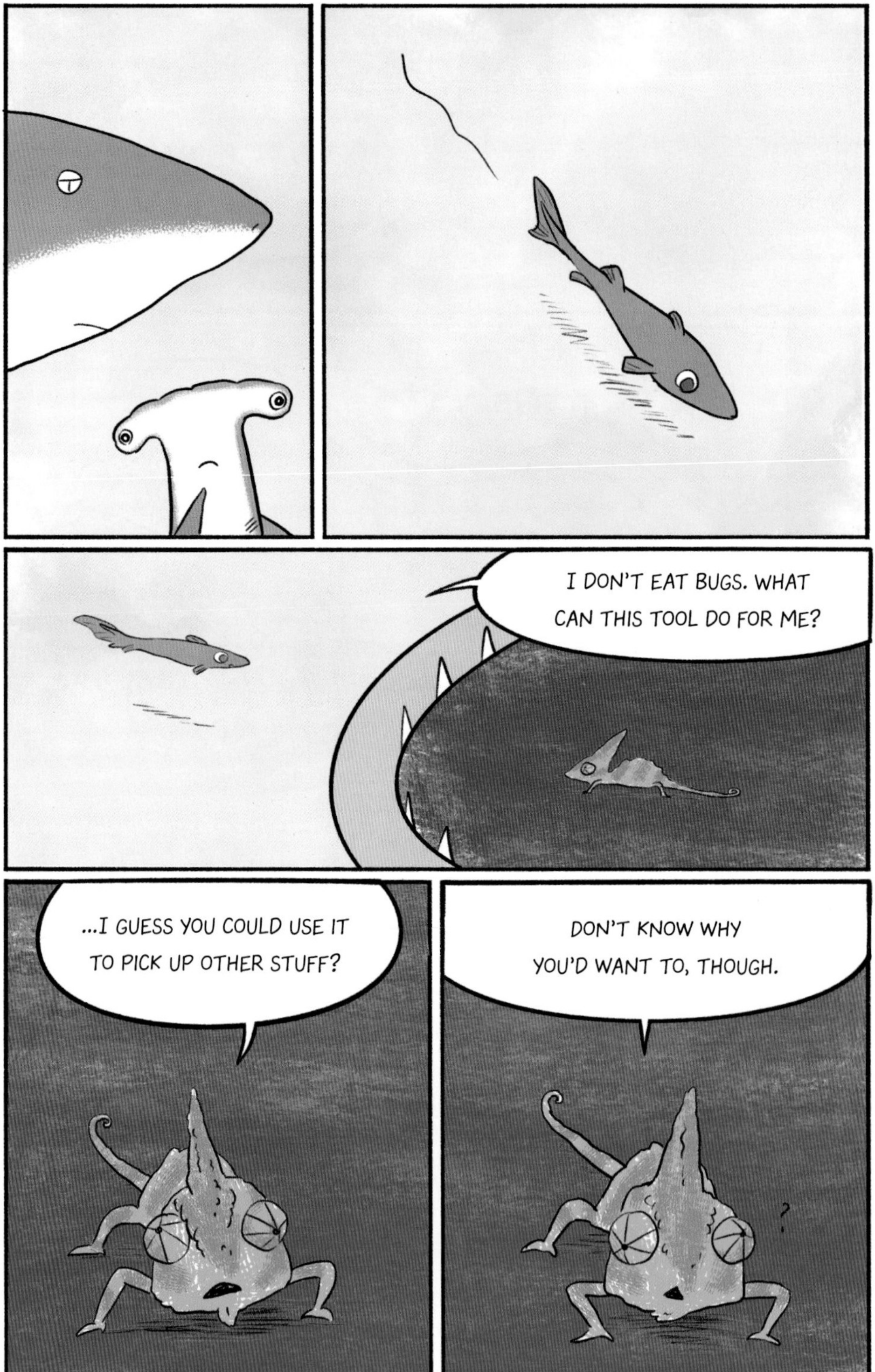
I DON'T EAT BUGS. WHAT CAN THIS TOOL DO FOR ME?
...I GUESS YOU COULD USE IT TO PICK UP OTHER STUFF?
DON'T KNOW WHY YOU'D WANT TO, THOUGH.

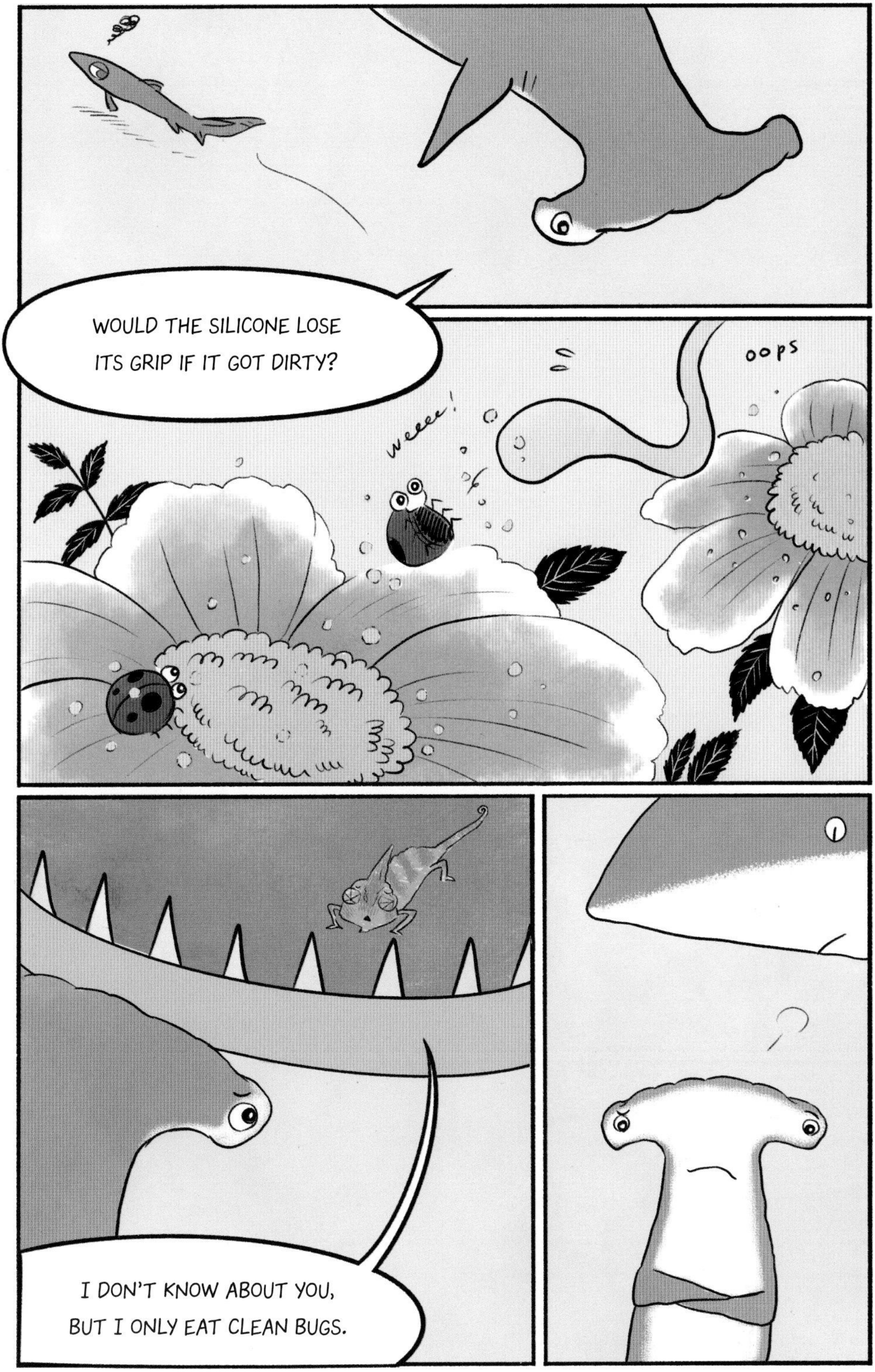
WOULD THE SILICONE LOSE ITS GRIP IF IT GOT DIRTY?
weeee!
oops
I DON'T KNOW ABOUT YOU, BUT I ONLY EAT CLEAN BUGS.

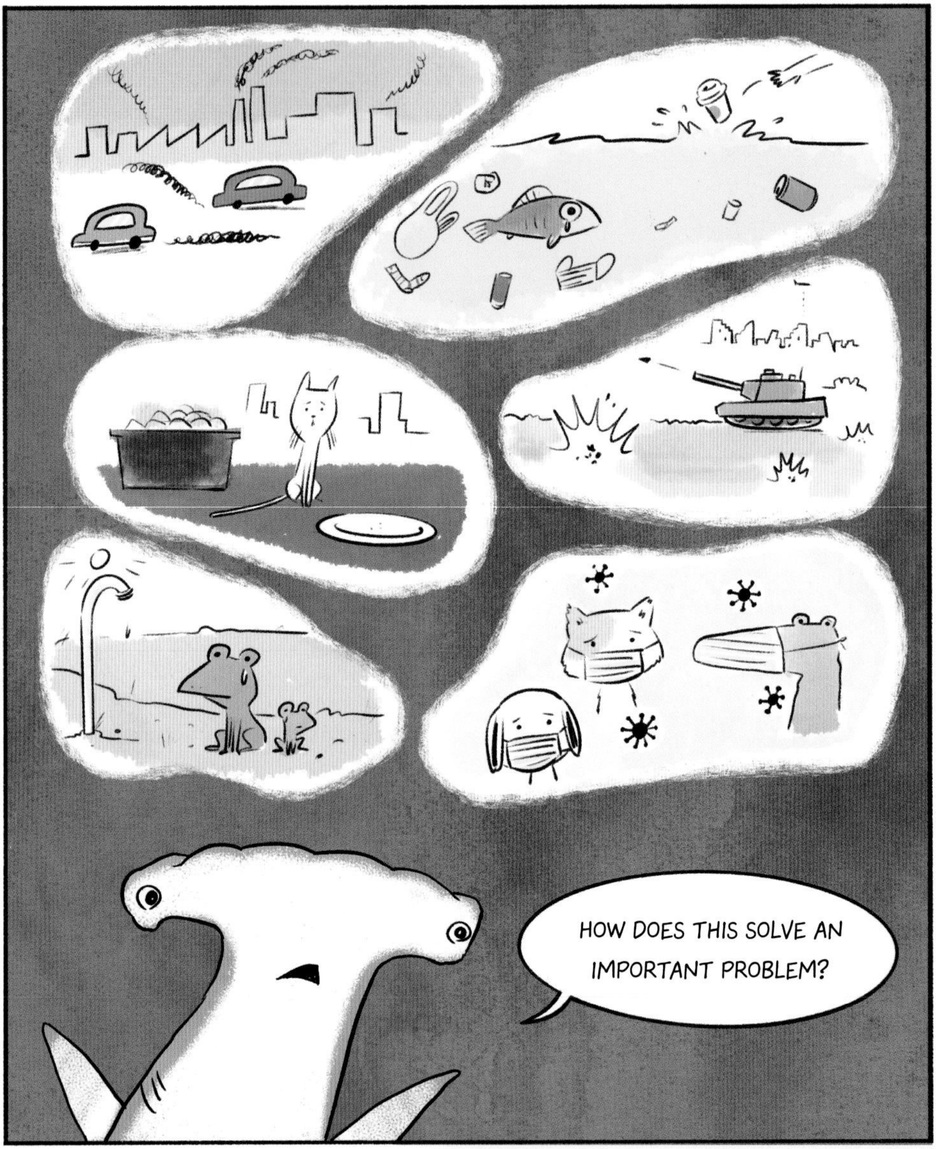
HOW DOES THIS SOLVE AN IMPORTANT PROBLEM?

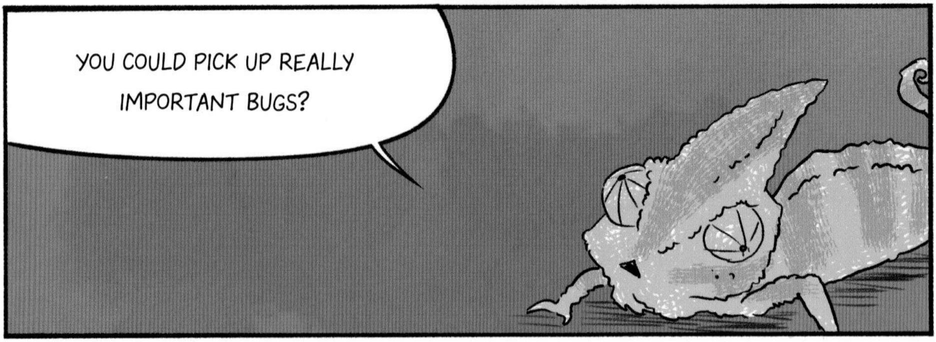
YOU COULD PICK UP REALLY IMPORTANT BUGS?

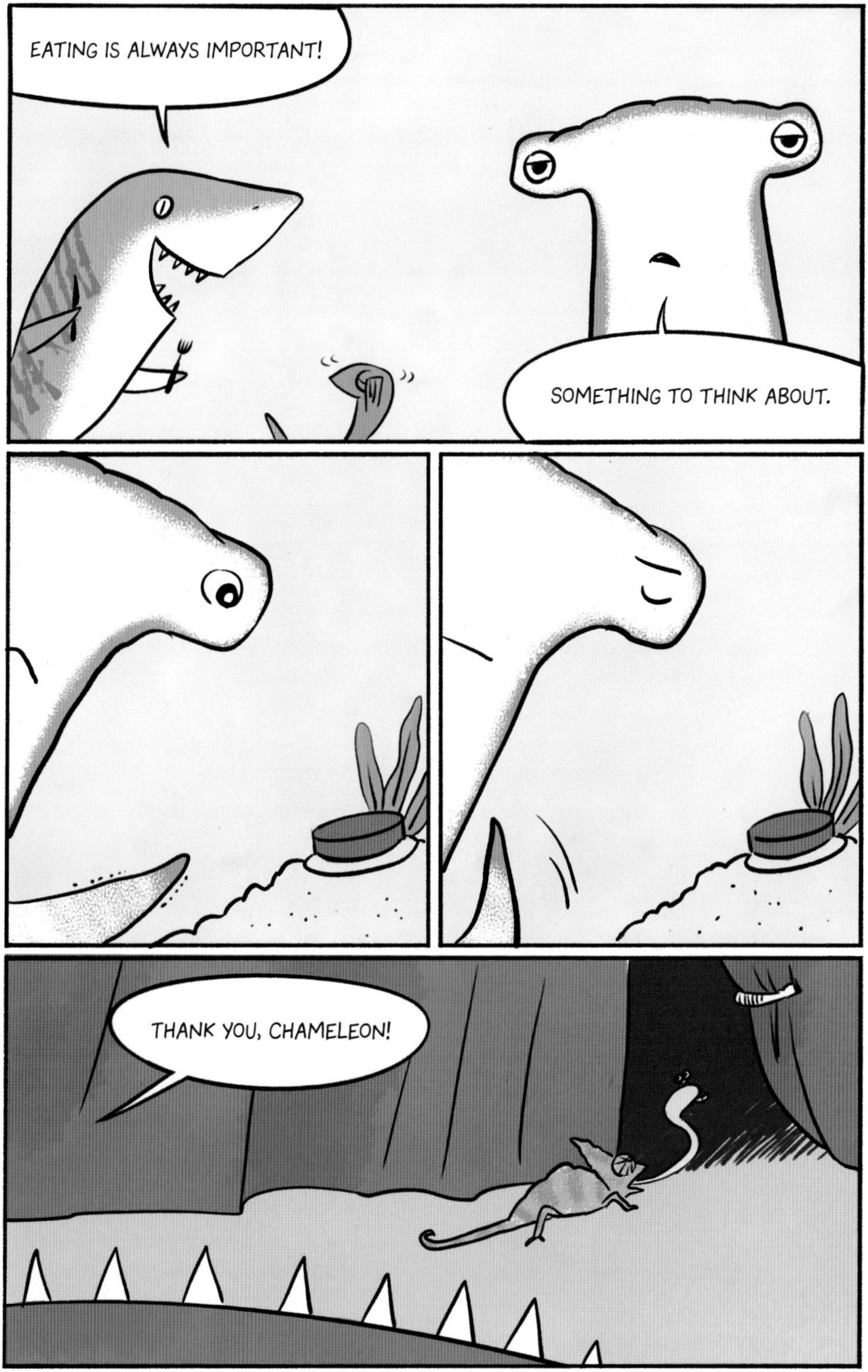
EATING IS ALWAYS IMPORTANT!
SOMETHING TO THINK ABOUT.
THANK YOU, CHAMELEON!

CHAPTER
THREE

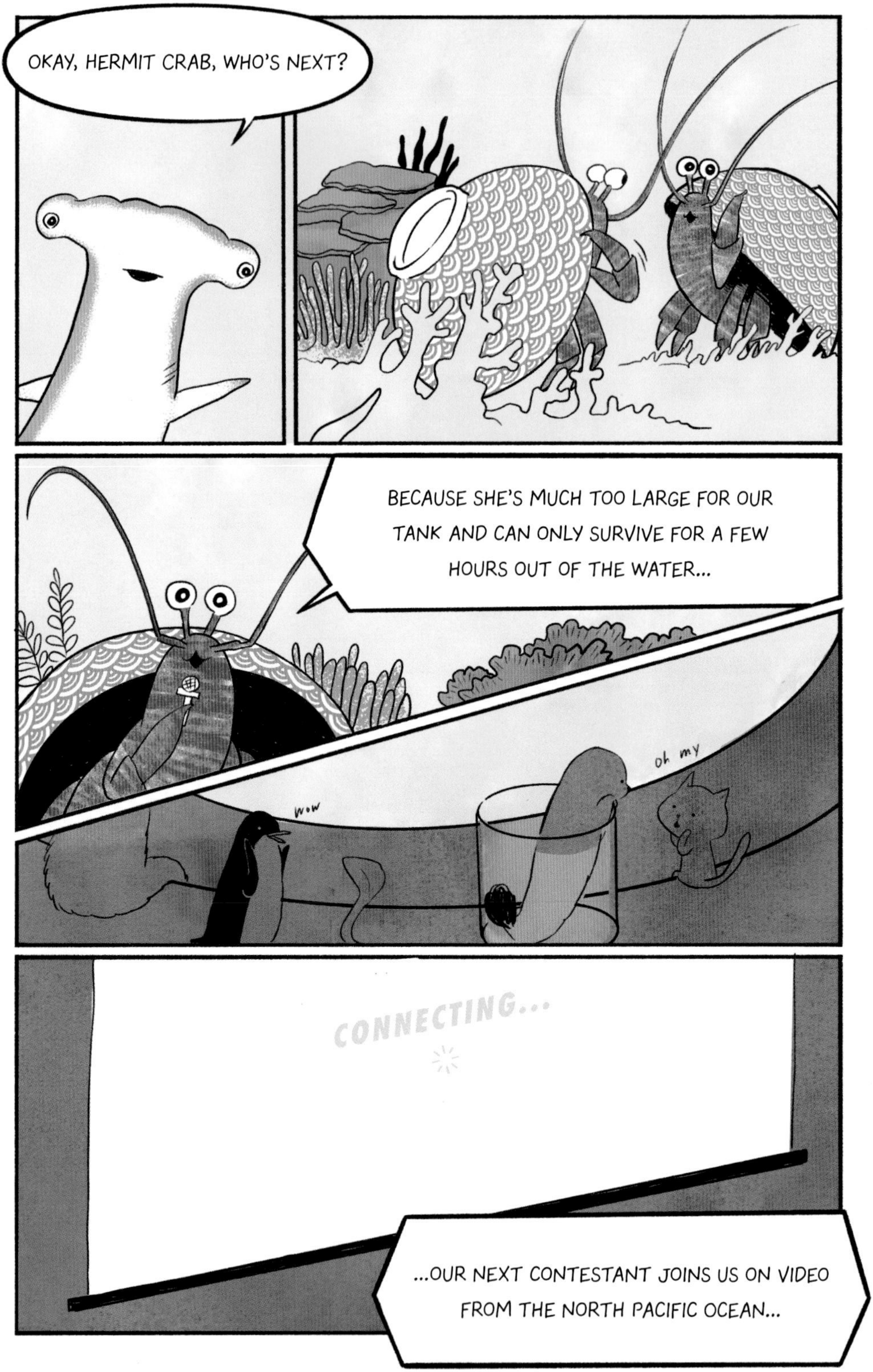
OKAY, HERMIT CRAB, WHO'S NEXT?
BECAUSE SHE'S MUCH TOO LARGE FOR OUR TANK AND CAN ONLY SURVIVE FOR A FEW HOURS OUT OF THE WATER...
wow
oh my
CONNECTING...
...OUR NEXT CONTESTANT JOINS US ON VIDEO FROM THE NORTH PACIFIC OCEAN...

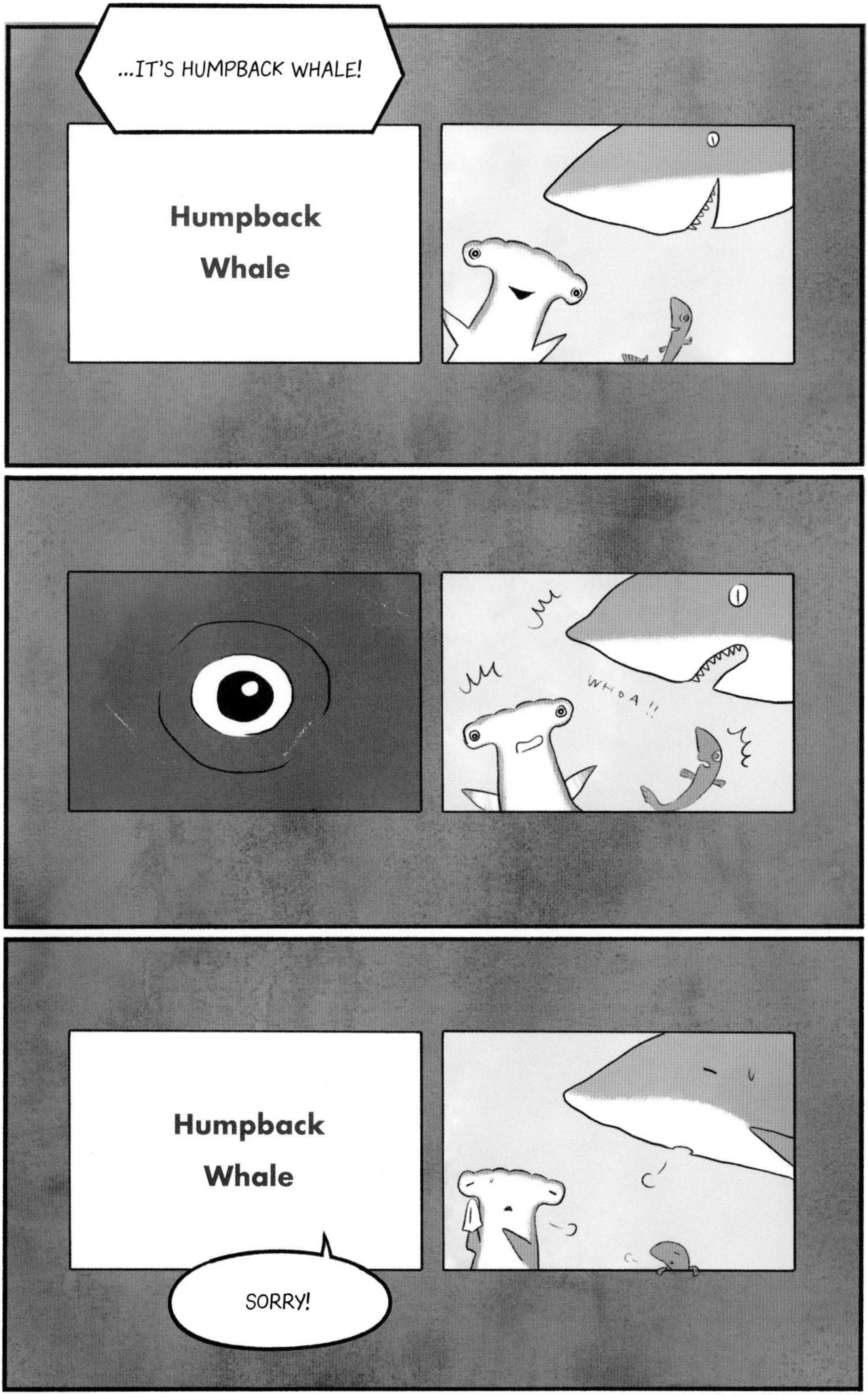
...IT'S HUMPBACK WHALE!
Humpback Whale
WHOA!!
Humpback Whale
SORRY!

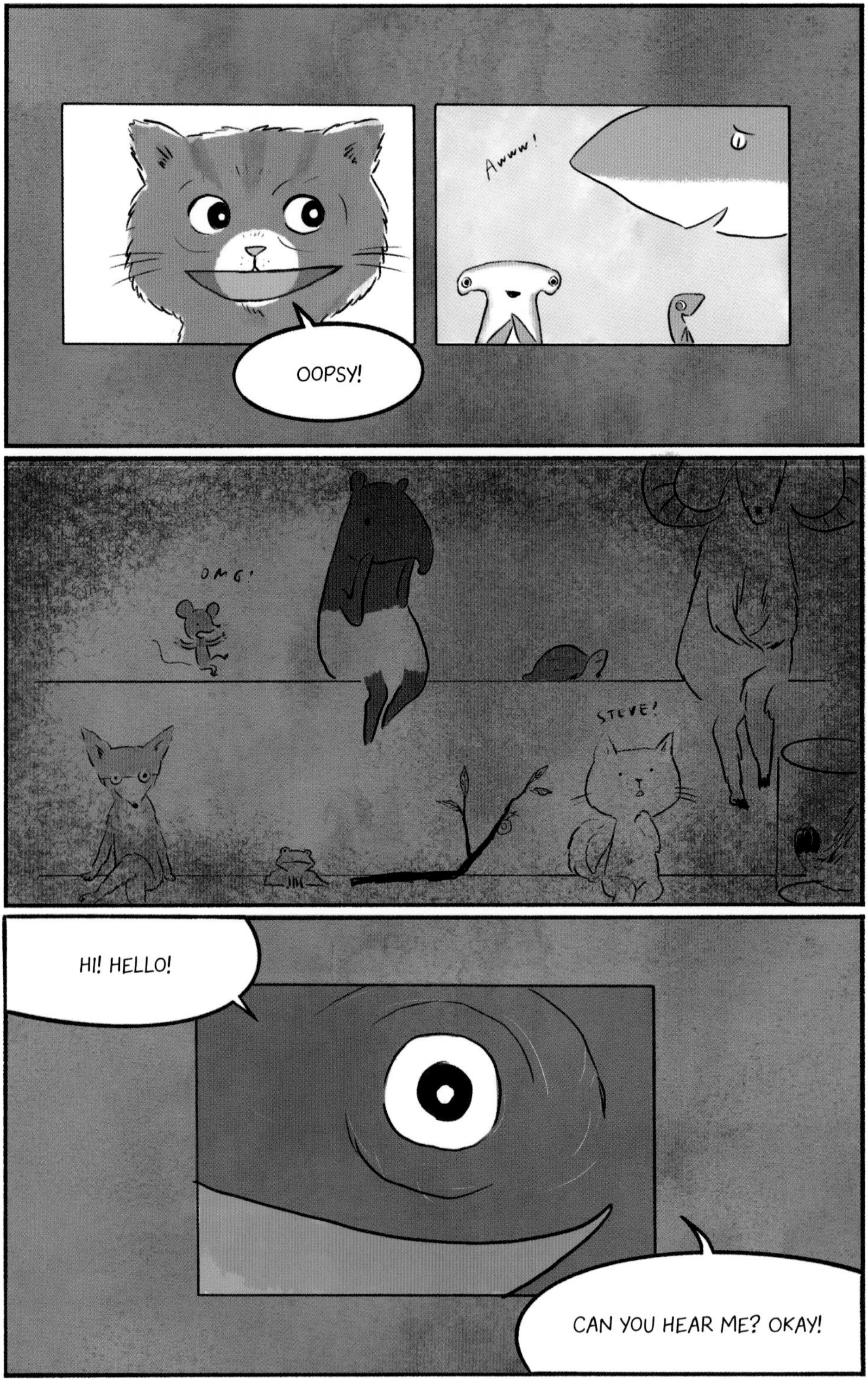
OOPSY!
Awww!
OMG!
STEVE!
HI! HELLO!
CAN YOU HEAR ME? OKAY!

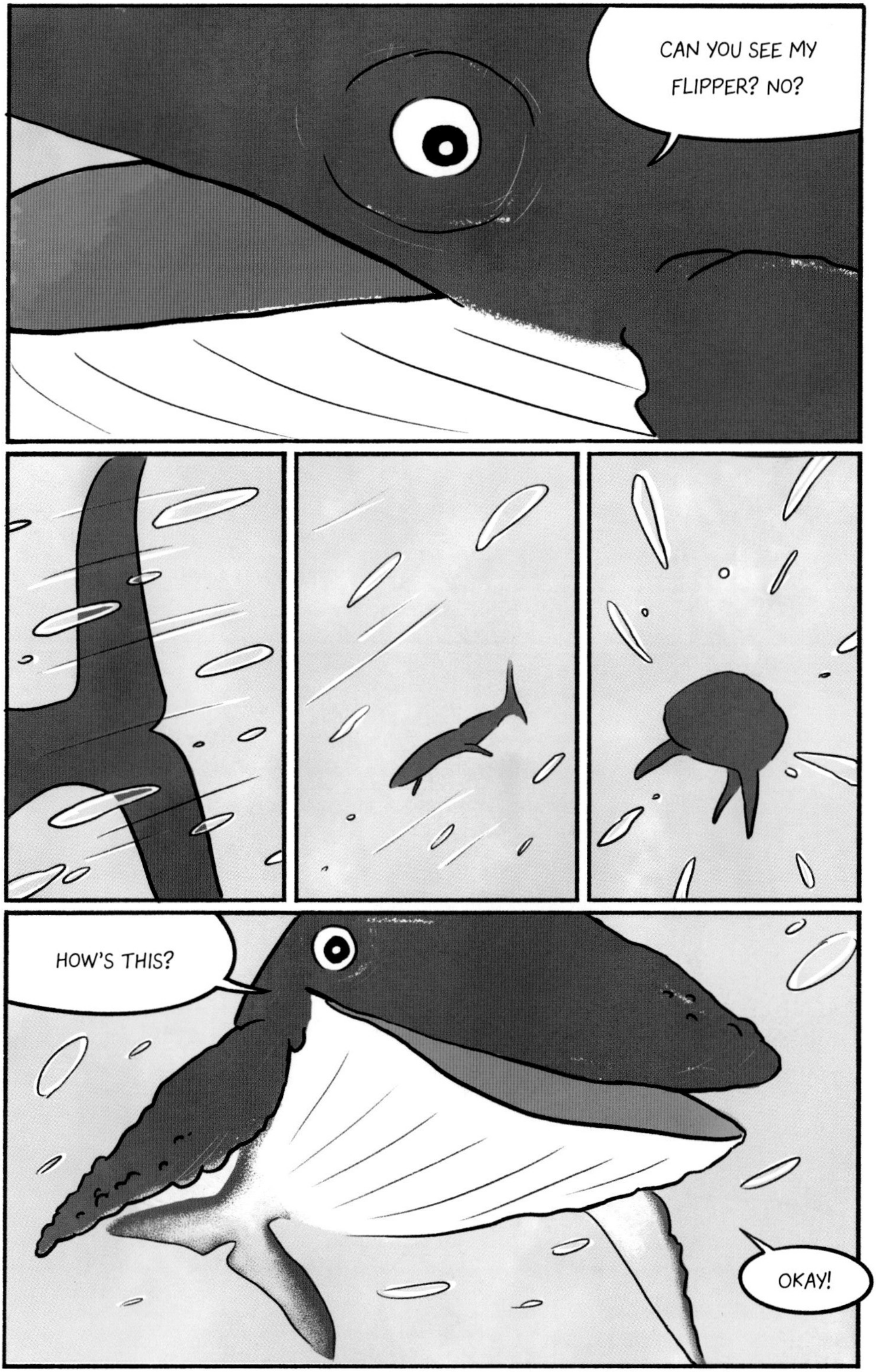
CAN YOU SEE MY FLIPPER? NO?
HOW'S THIS?
OKAY!

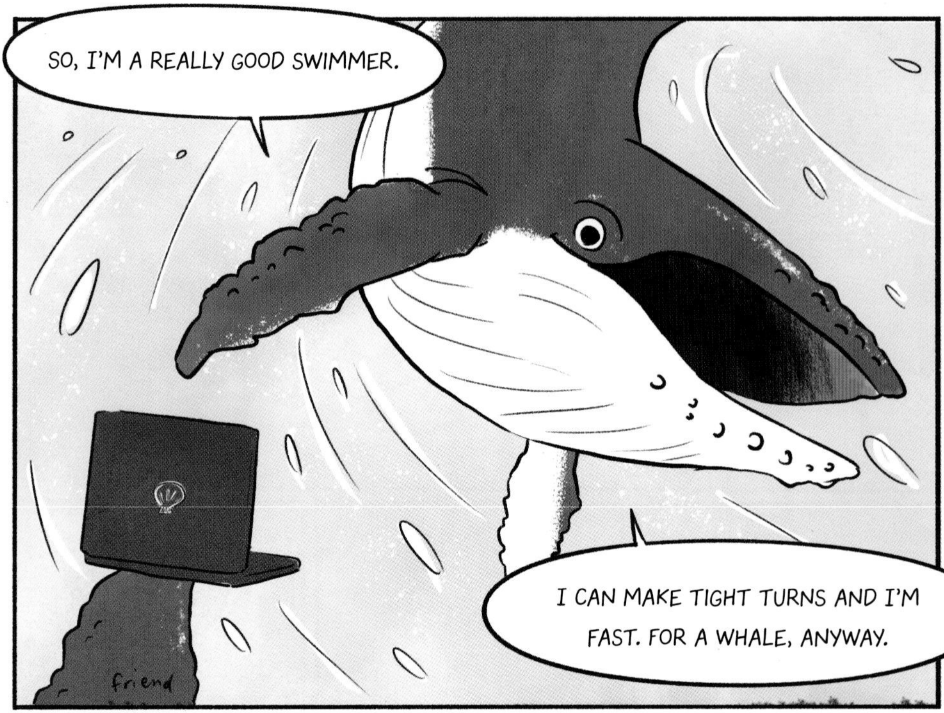
SO, I'M A REALLY GOOD SWIMMER.
I CAN MAKE TIGHT TURNS AND I'M FAST. FOR A WHALE, ANYWAY.
friend

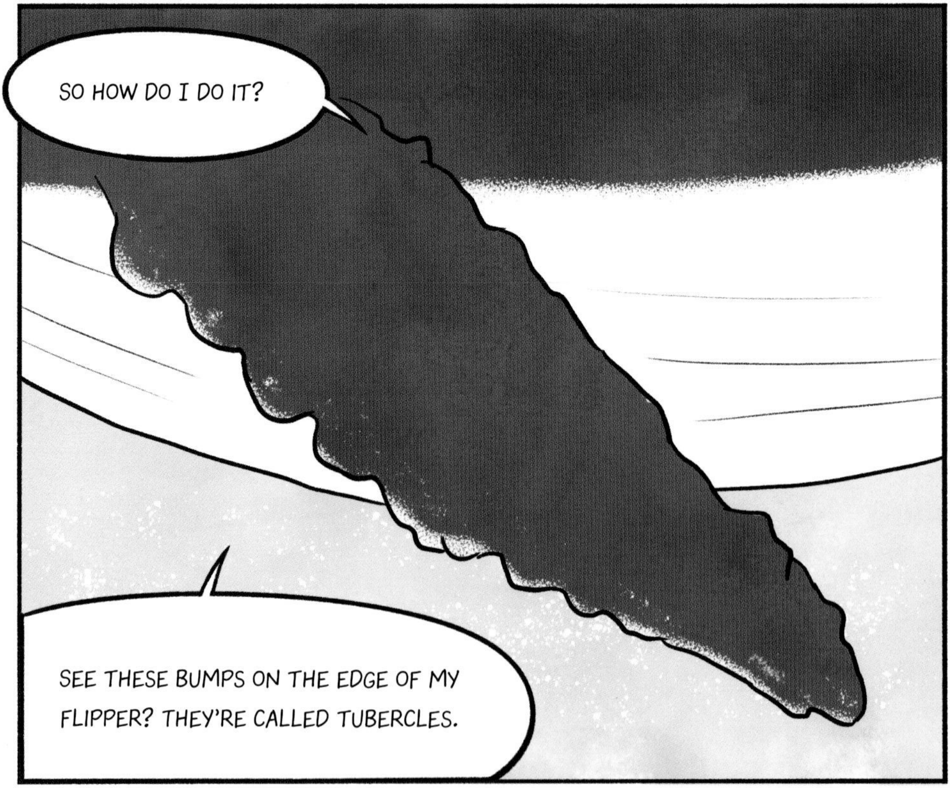
SO HOW DO I DO IT?
SEE THESE BUMPS ON THE EDGE OF MY FLIPPER? THEY'RE CALLED TUBERCLES.

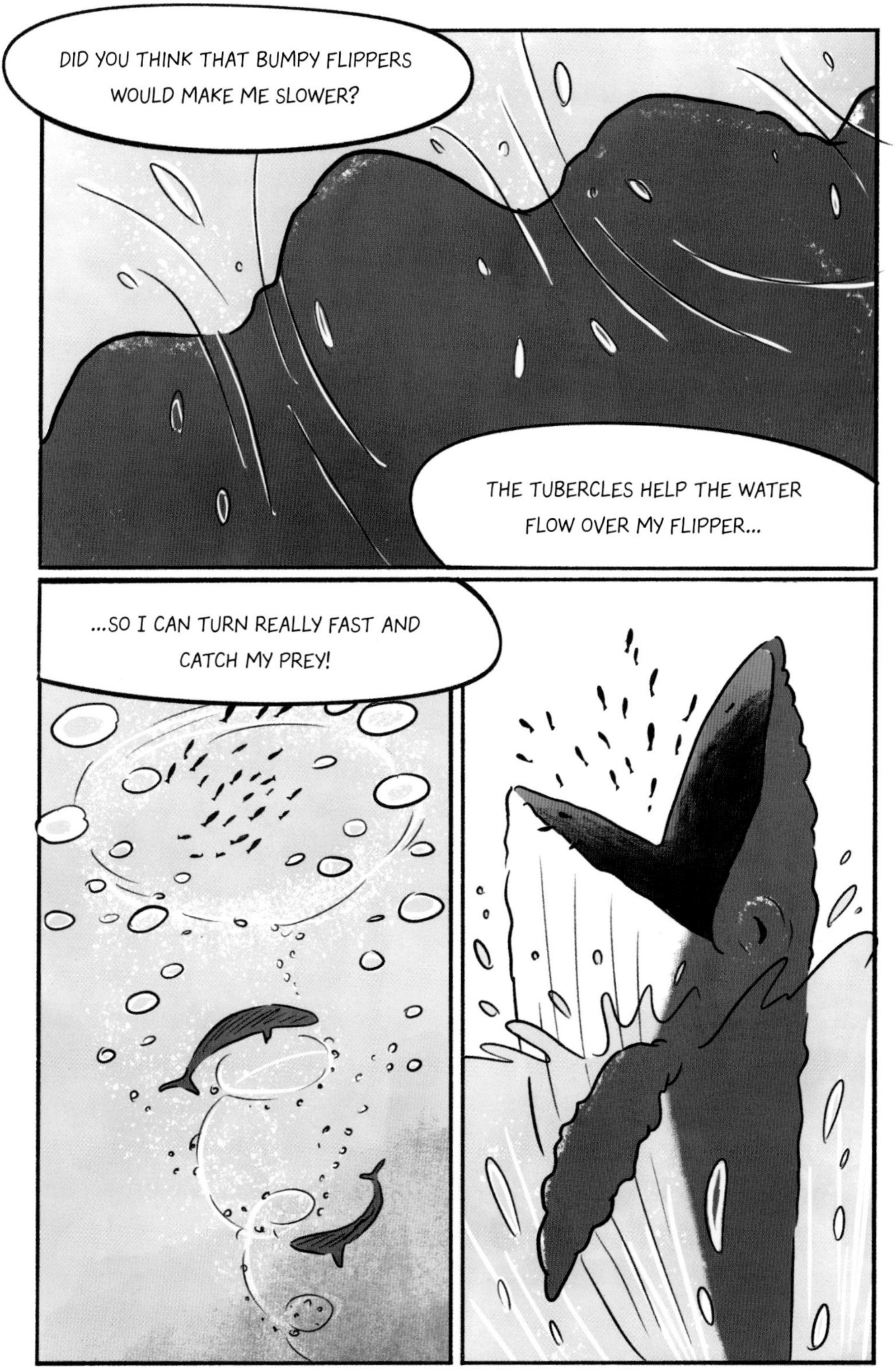
DID YOU THINK THAT BUMPY FLIPPERS WOULD MAKE ME SLOWER?
THE TUBERCLES HELP THE WATER FLOW OVER MY FLIPPER...
...SO I CAN TURN REALLY FAST AND CATCH MY PREY!

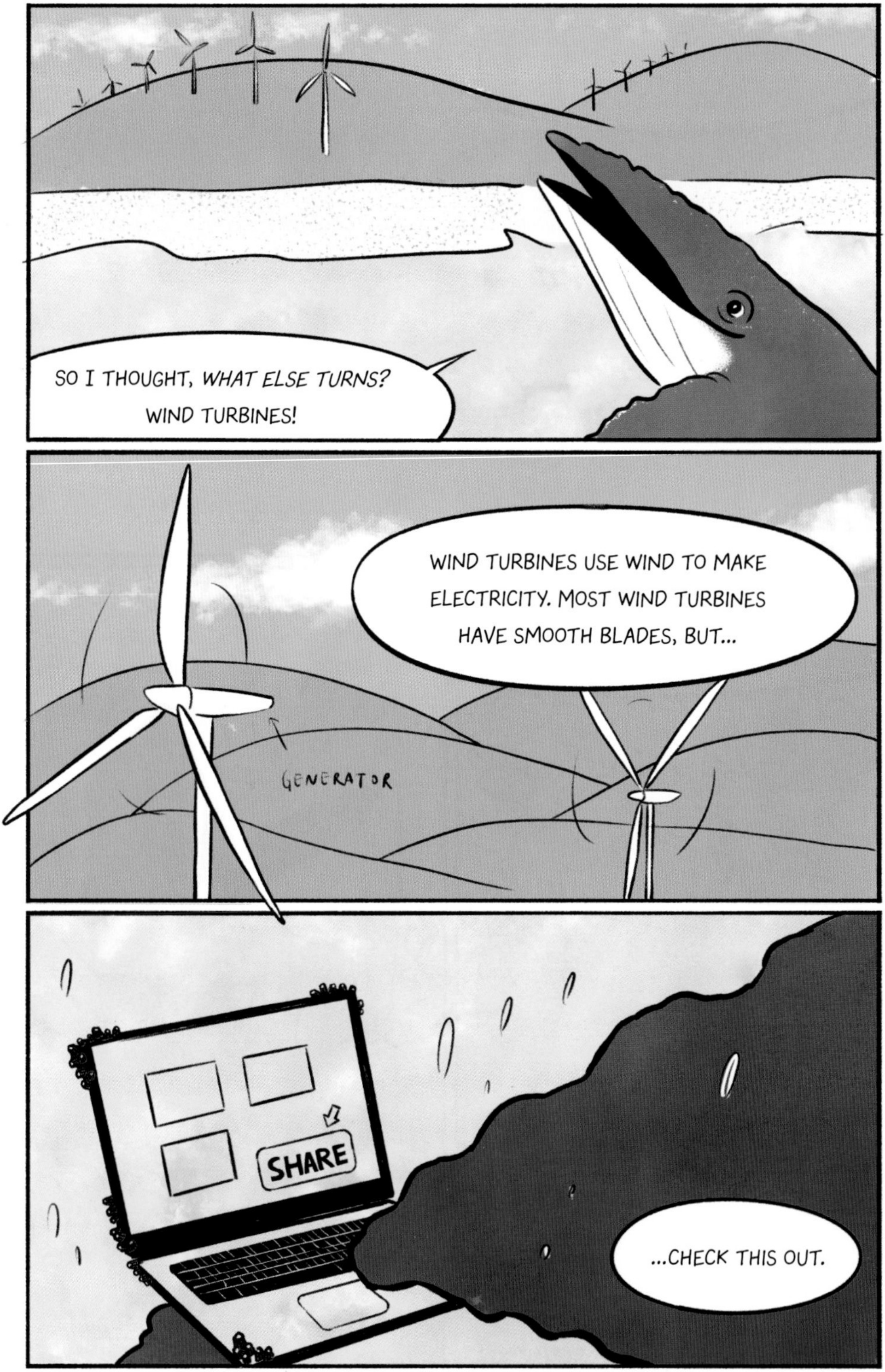

SO I THOUGHT, *WHAT ELSE TURNS?* WIND TURBINES!
WIND TURBINES USE WIND TO MAKE ELECTRICITY. MOST WIND TURBINES HAVE SMOOTH BLADES, BUT...
GENERATOR
SHARE
...CHECK THIS OUT.

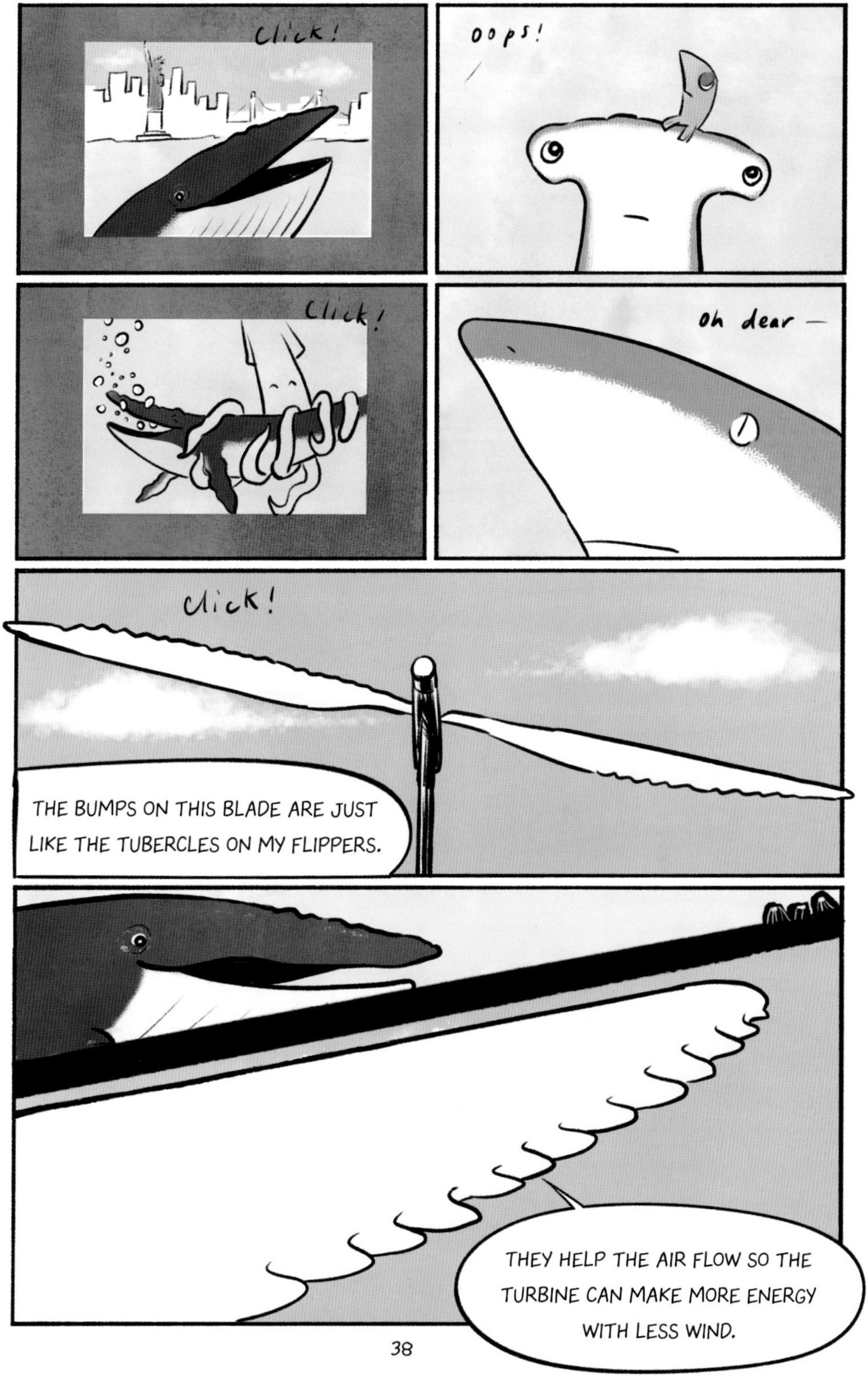
click!
oops!
click!
oh dear —
click!
THE BUMPS ON THIS BLADE ARE JUST LIKE THE TUBERCLES ON MY FLIPPERS.
THEY HELP THE AIR FLOW SO THE TURBINE CAN MAKE MORE ENERGY WITH LESS WIND.

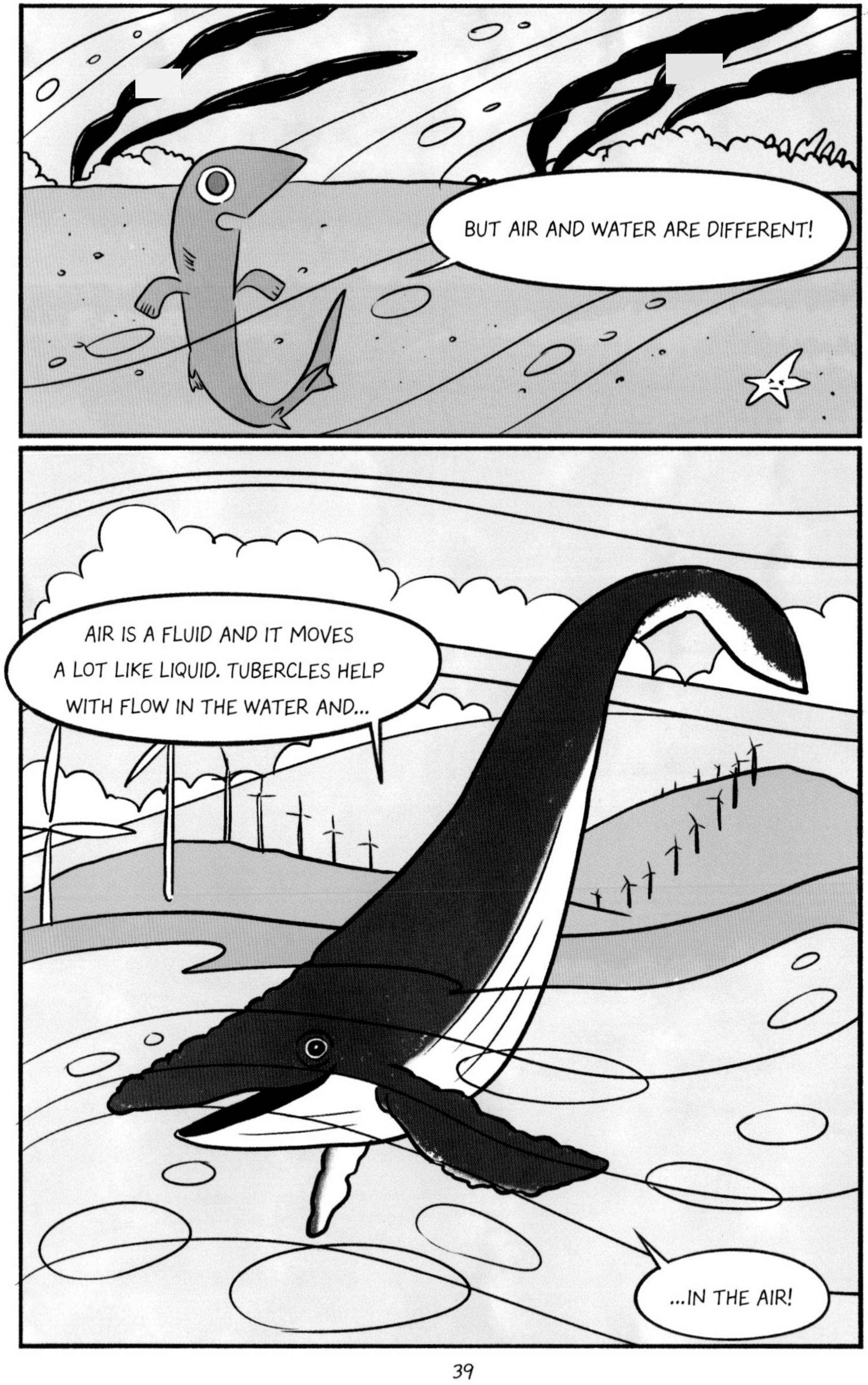
BUT AIR AND WATER ARE DIFFERENT!
AIR IS A FLUID AND IT MOVES A LOT LIKE LIQUID. TUBERCLES HELP WITH FLOW IN THE WATER AND...
...IN THE AIR!

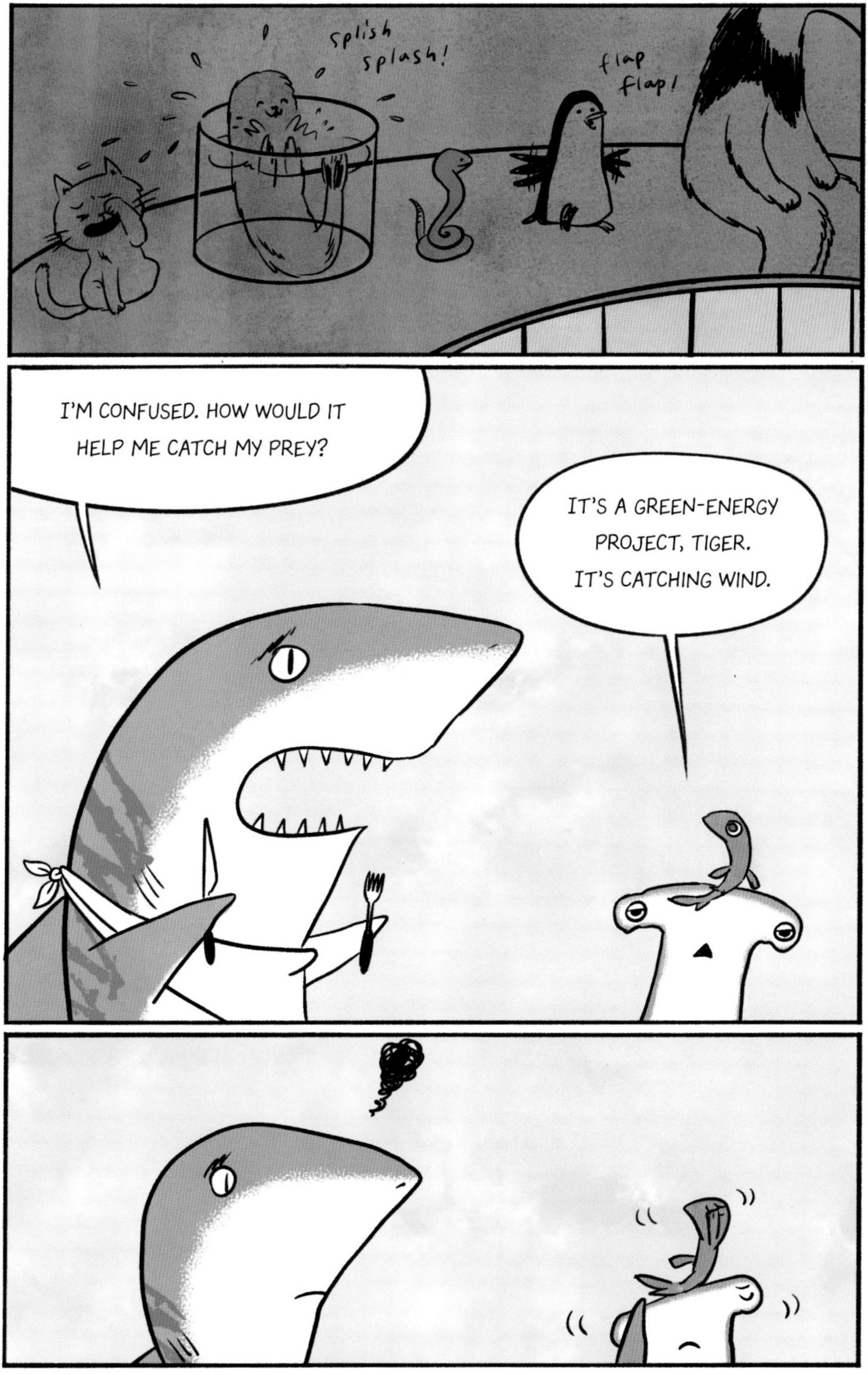
splish
splash!
flap
flap!
I'M CONFUSED. HOW WOULD IT HELP ME CATCH MY PREY?
IT'S A GREEN-ENERGY PROJECT, TIGER. IT'S CATCHING WIND.

CHAPTER
FOUR

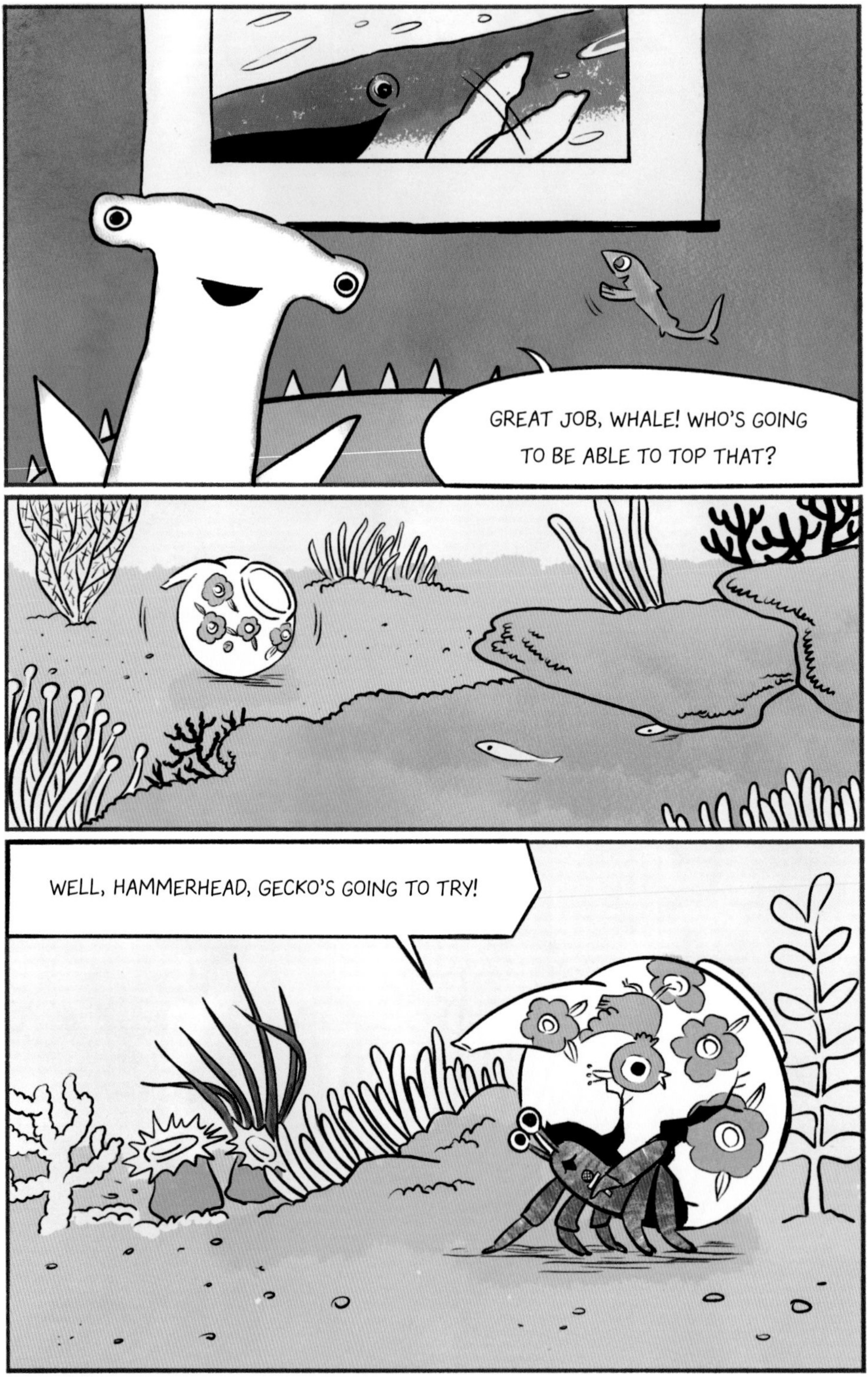
GREAT JOB, WHALE! WHO'S GOING TO BE ABLE TO TOP THAT?
WELL, HAMMERHEAD, GECKO'S GOING TO TRY!

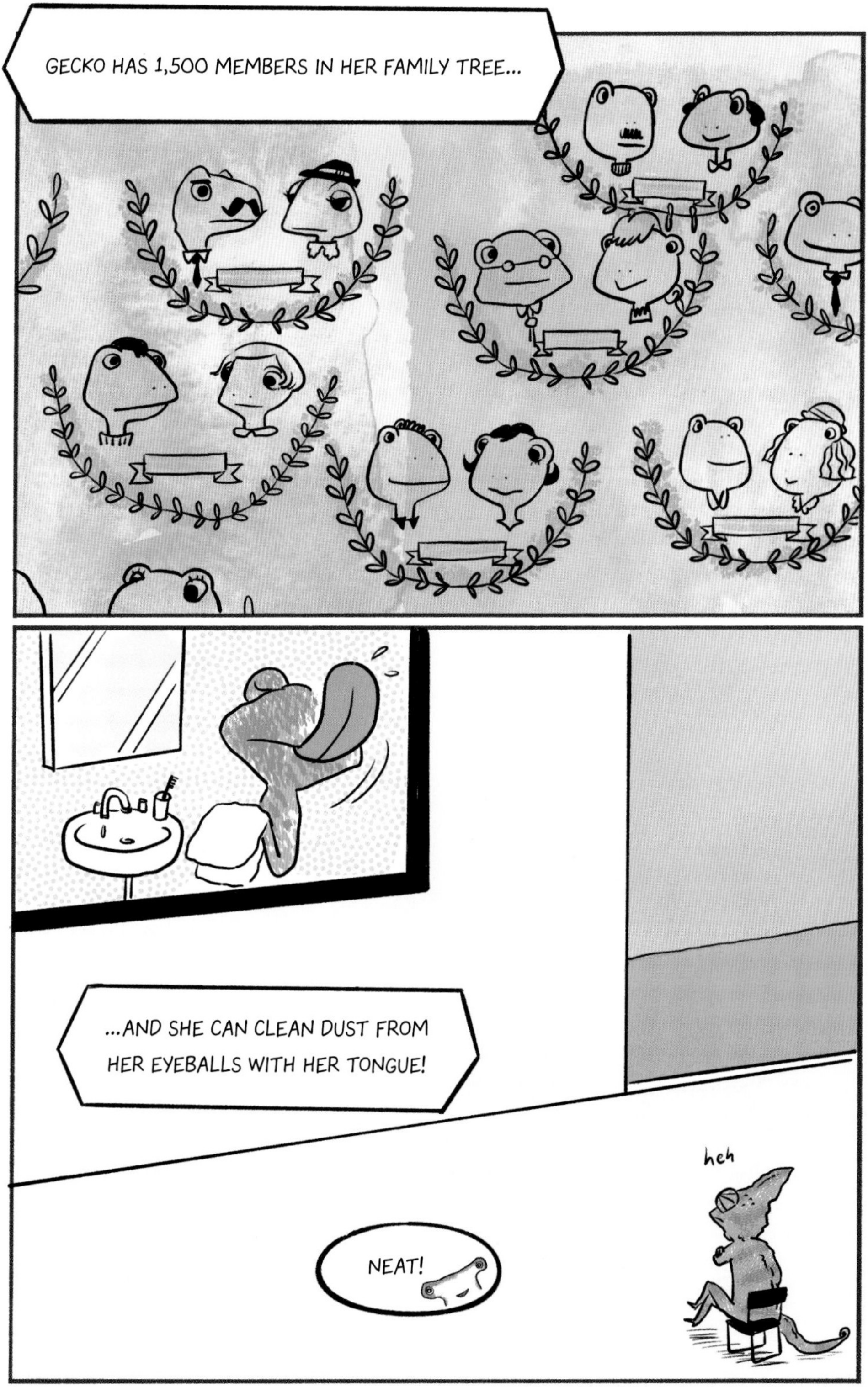
GECKO HAS 1,500 MEMBERS IN HER FAMILY TREE...
...AND SHE CAN CLEAN DUST FROM HER EYEBALLS WITH HER TONGUE!
heh
NEAT!

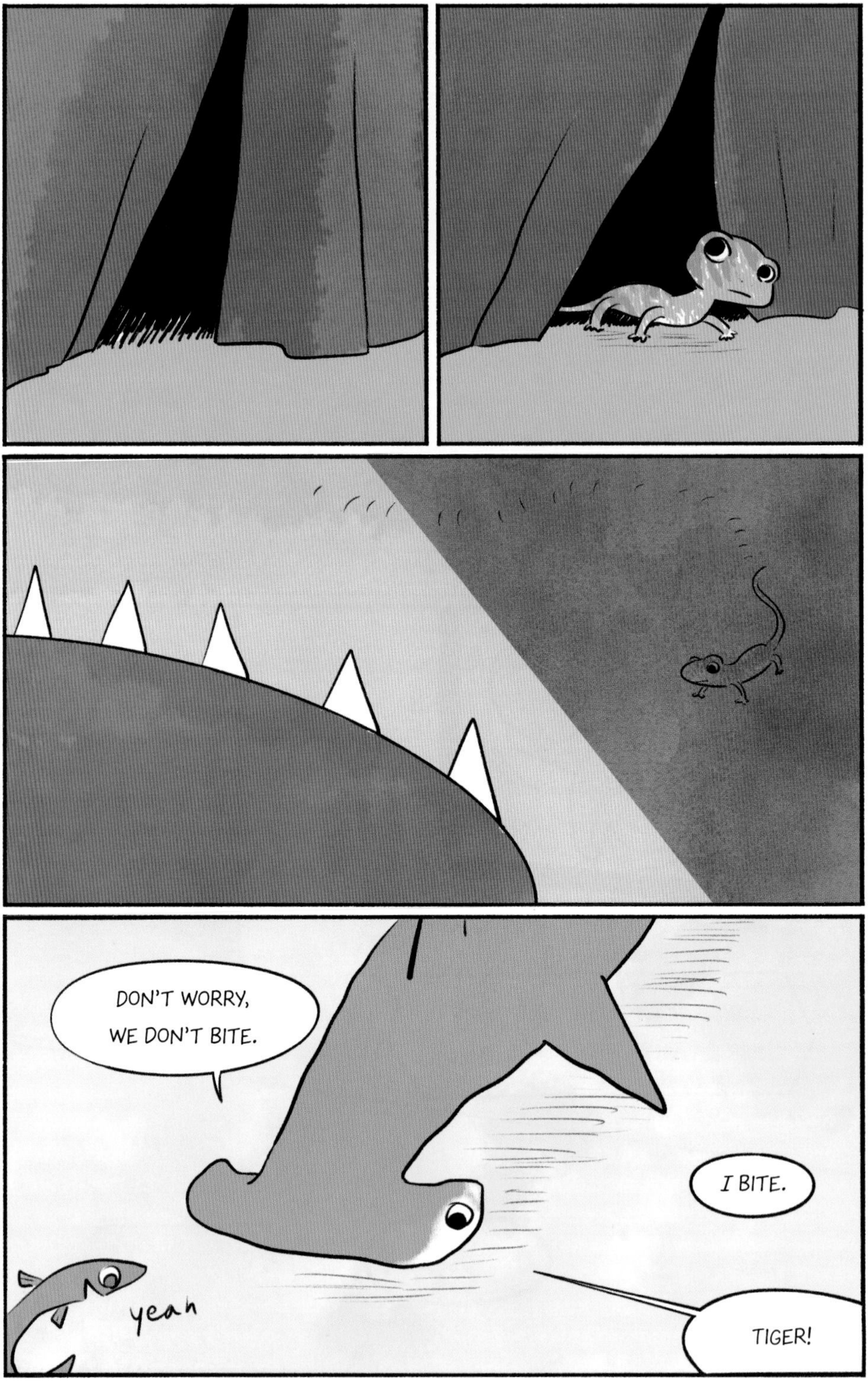
DON'T WORRY,
WE DON'T BITE.
I BITE.
yeah
TIGER!

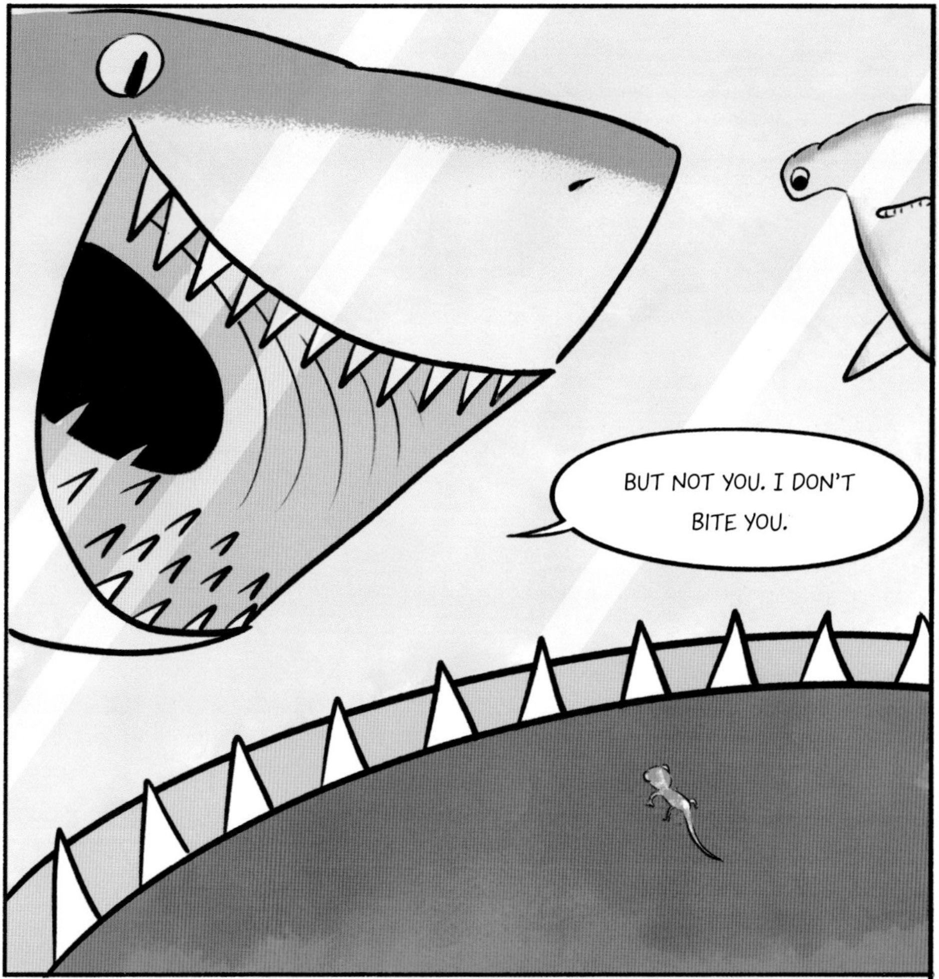
BUT NOT YOU. I DON'T BITE YOU.

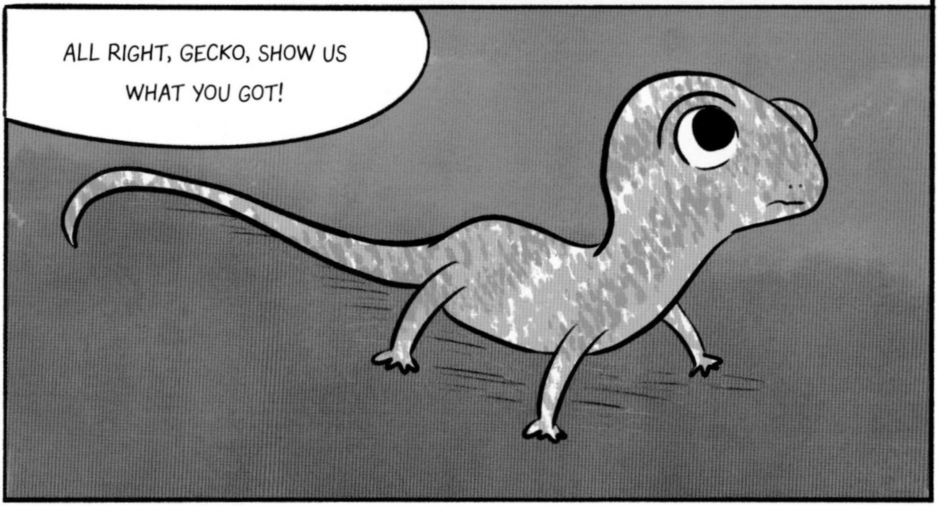
ALL RIGHT, GECKO, SHOW US WHAT YOU GOT!

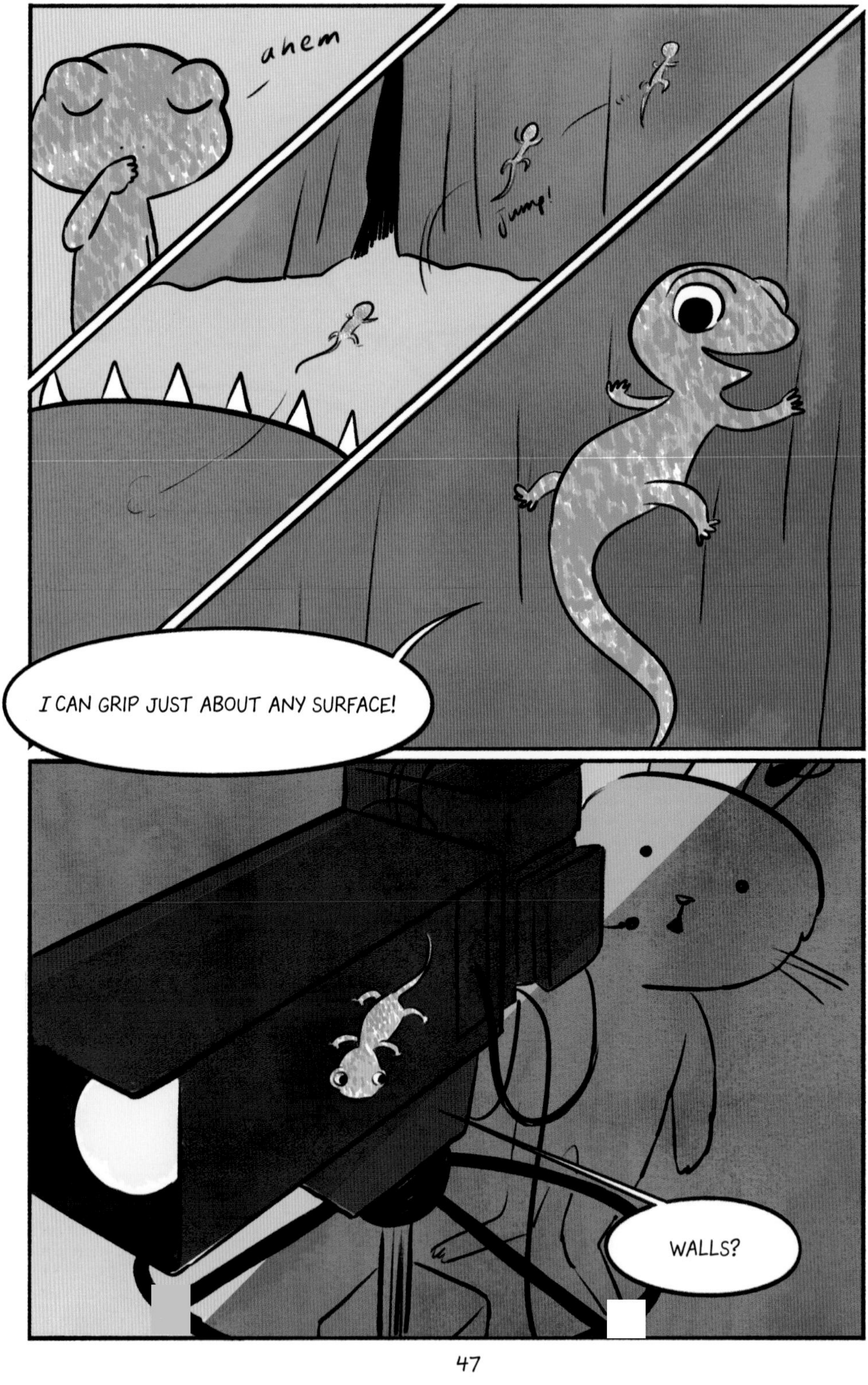
ahem
Jump!
I CAN GRIP JUST ABOUT ANY SURFACE!
WALLS?

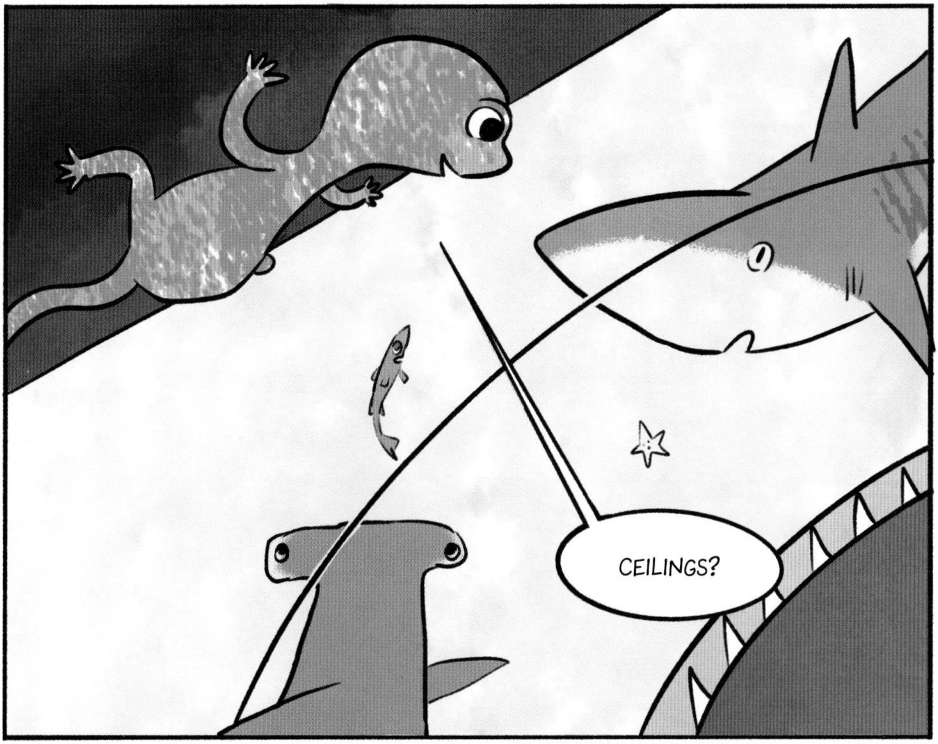
CEILINGS?

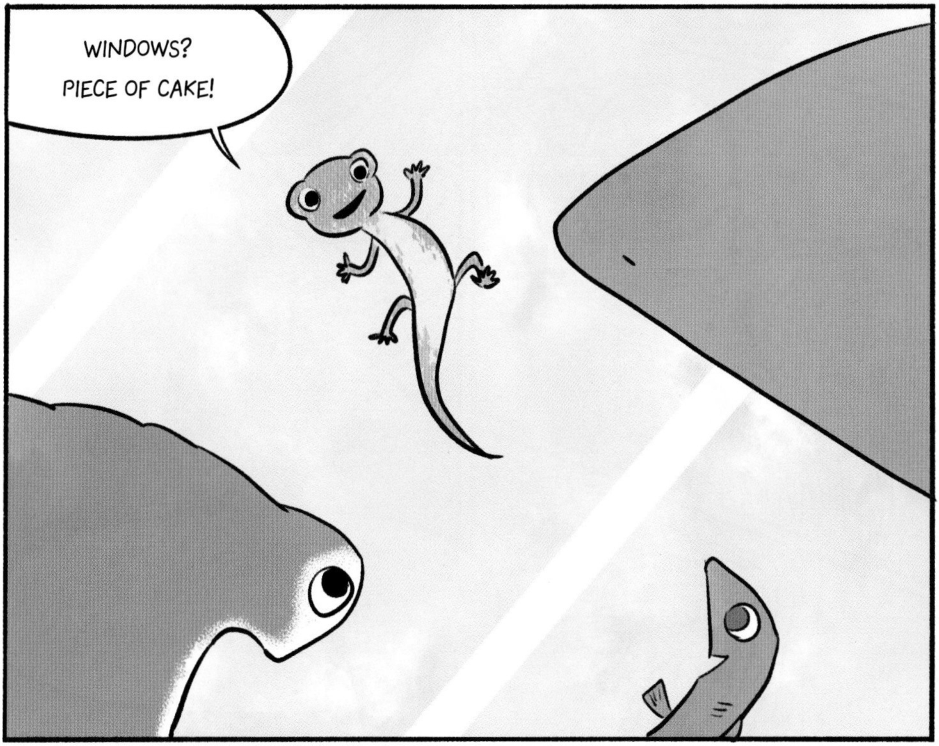
WINDOWS?
PIECE OF CAKE!

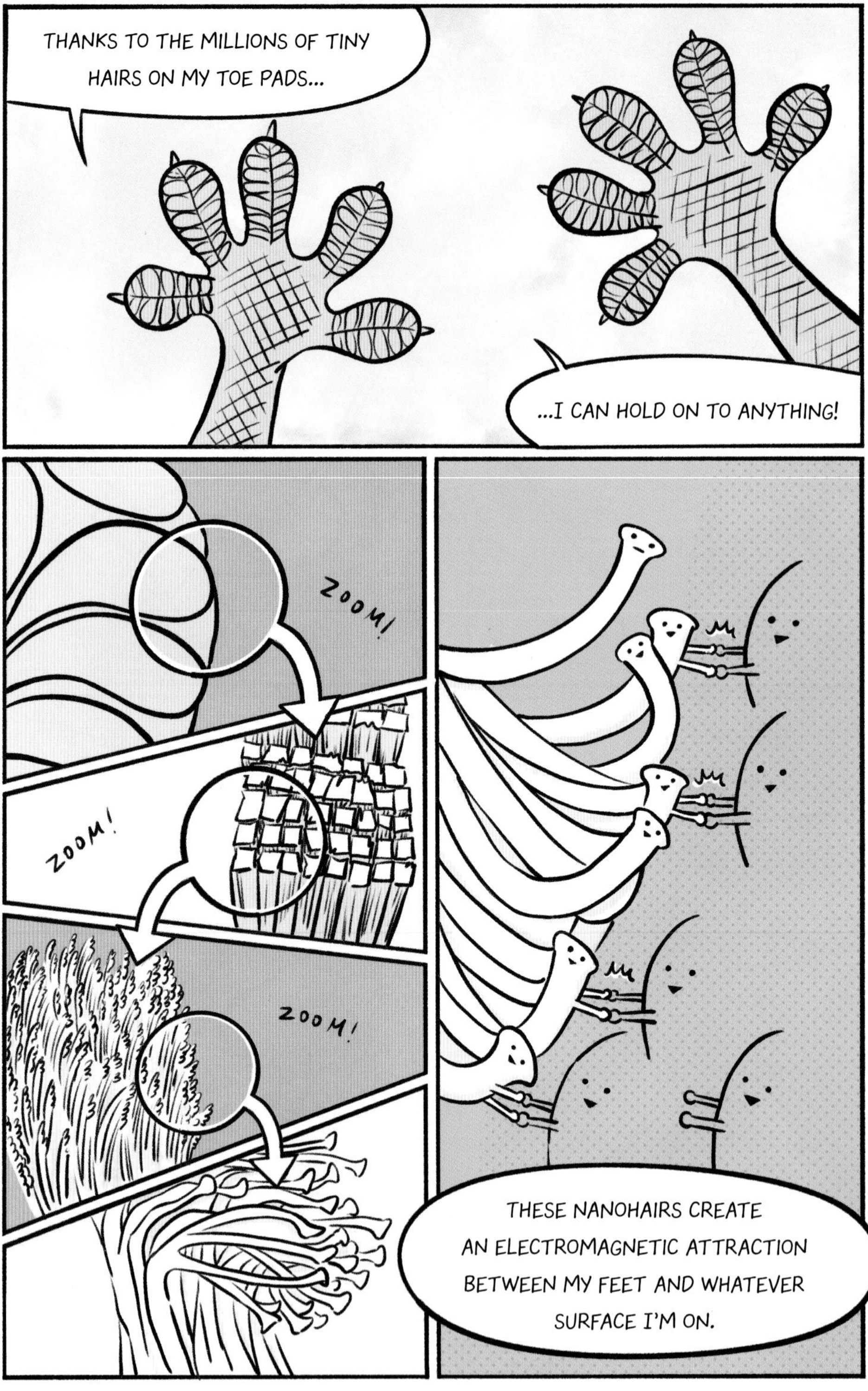
THANKS TO THE MILLIONS OF TINY HAIRS ON MY TOE PADS...
...I CAN HOLD ON TO ANYTHING!
ZOOM!
ZOOM!
ZOOM!
THESE NANOHAIRS CREATE AN ELECTROMAGNETIC ATTRACTION BETWEEN MY FEET AND WHATEVER SURFACE I'M ON.

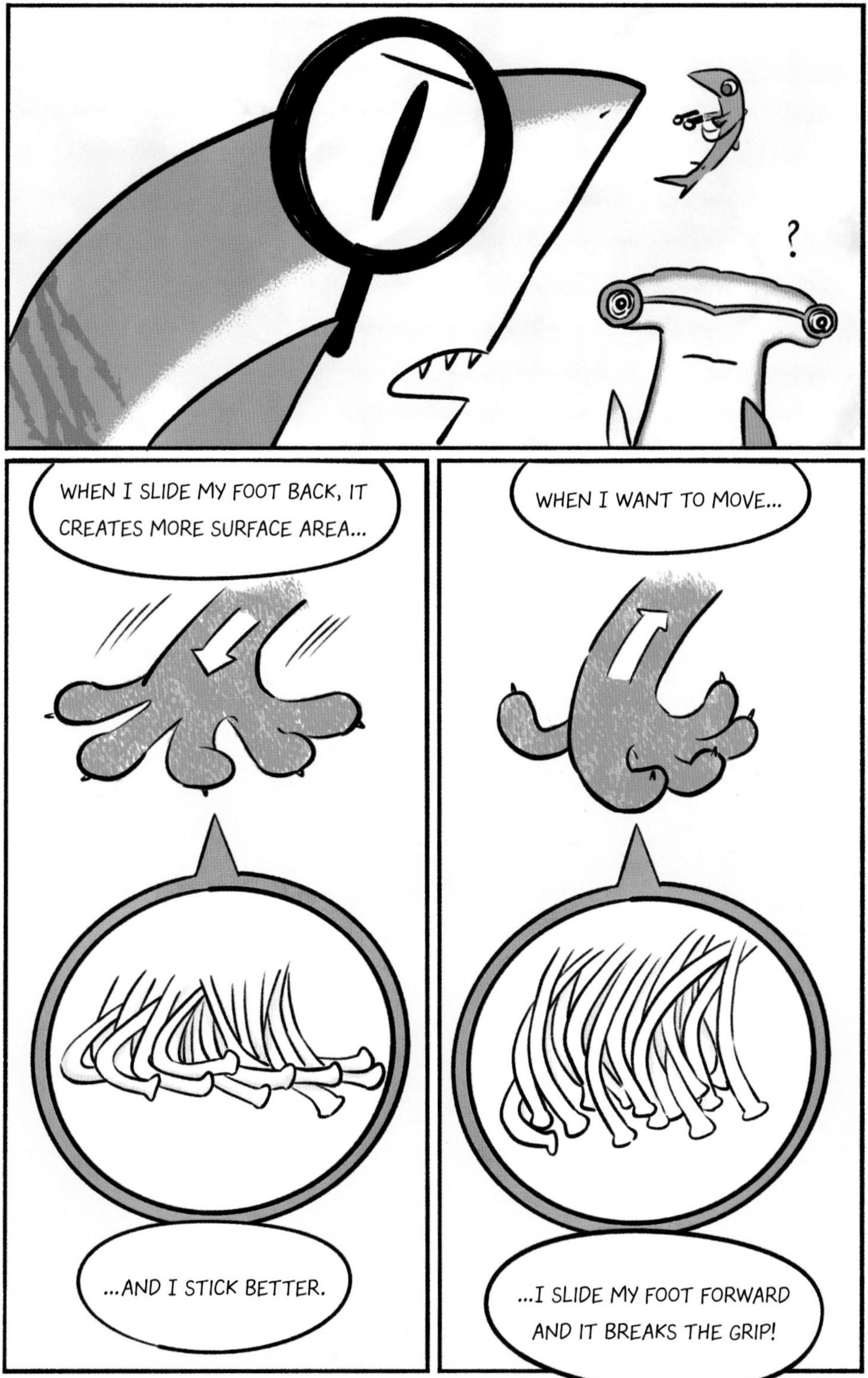
?
WHEN I SLIDE MY FOOT BACK, IT CREATES MORE SURFACE AREA...
...AND I STICK BETTER.
WHEN I WANT TO MOVE...
...I SLIDE MY FOOT FORWARD AND IT BREAKS THE GRIP!

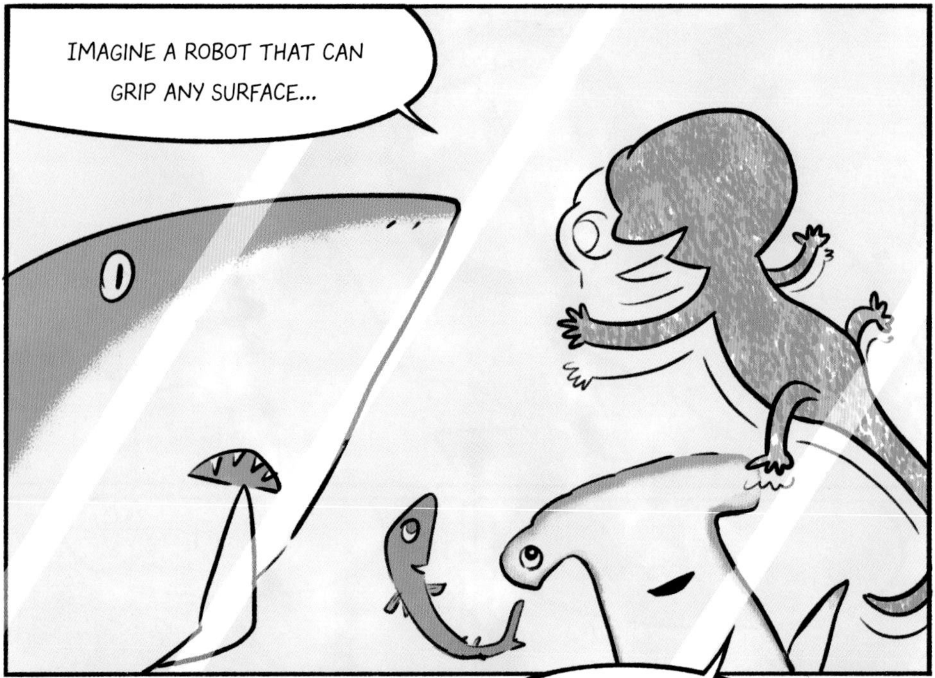
IMAGINE A ROBOT THAT CAN GRIP ANY SURFACE...

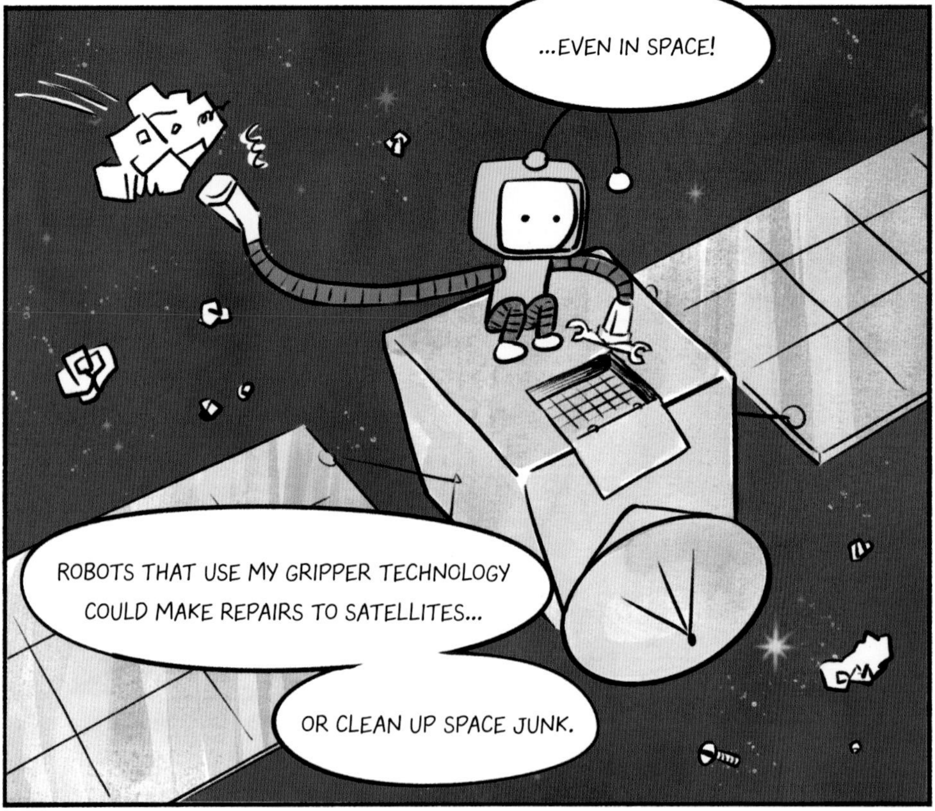
...EVEN IN SPACE!
ROBOTS THAT USE MY GRIPPER TECHNOLOGY COULD MAKE REPAIRS TO SATELLITES...
OR CLEAN UP SPACE JUNK.

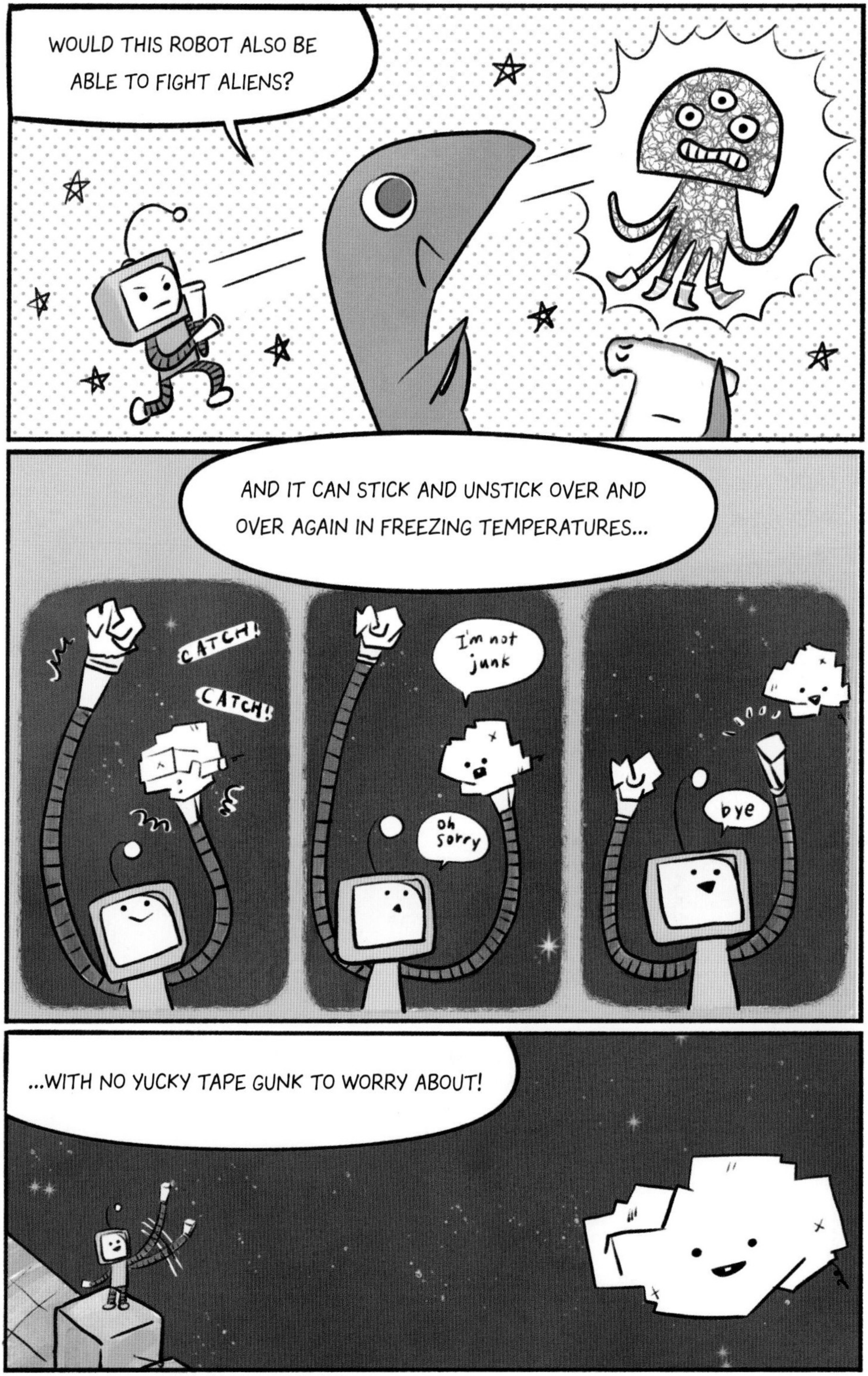
WOULD THIS ROBOT ALSO BE ABLE TO FIGHT ALIENS?
AND IT CAN STICK AND UNSTICK OVER AND OVER AGAIN IN FREEZING TEMPERATURES...
CATCH!
CATCH!
I'm not junk
Oh sorry
bye
...WITH NO YUCKY TAPE GUNK TO WORRY ABOUT!

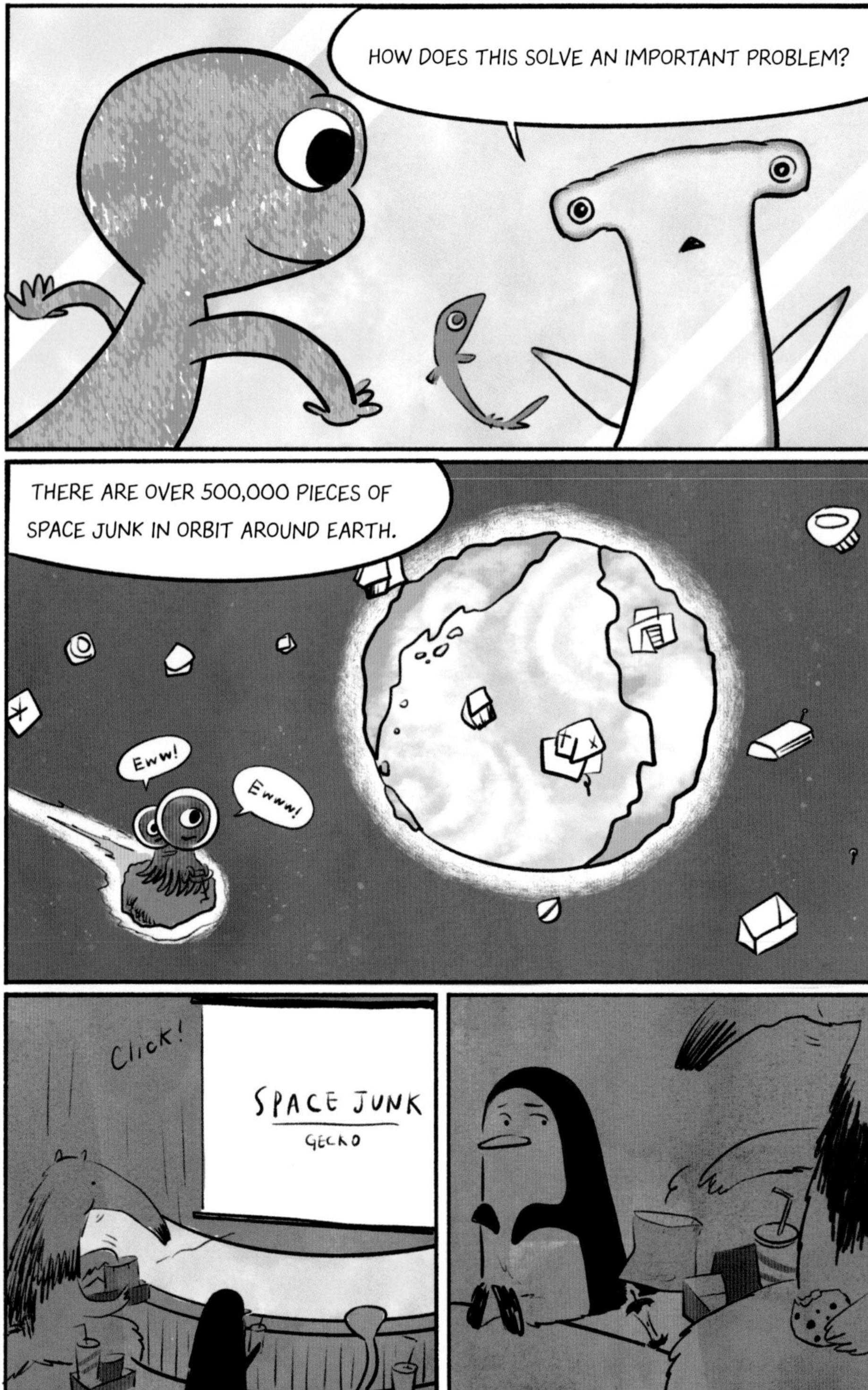
HOW DOES THIS SOLVE AN IMPORTANT PROBLEM?
THERE ARE OVER 500,000 PIECES OF SPACE JUNK IN ORBIT AROUND EARTH.
Eww!
Ewww!
Click!
SPACE JUNK
GECKO

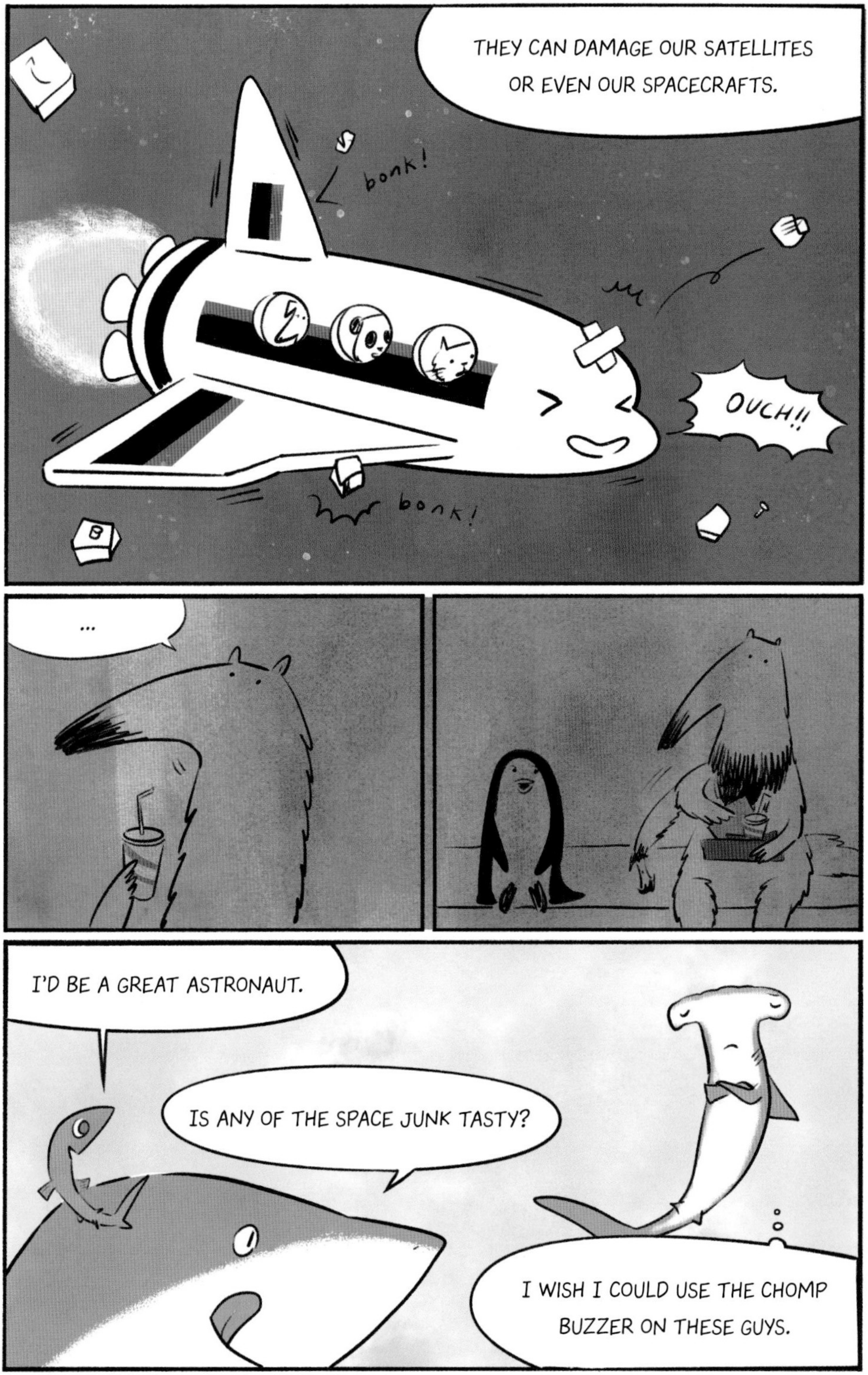
THEY CAN DAMAGE OUR SATELLITES OR EVEN OUR SPACECRAFTS.
bonk!
OUCH!!
bonk!
...
I'D BE A GREAT ASTRONAUT.
IS ANY OF THE SPACE JUNK TASTY?
I WISH I COULD USE THE CHOMP BUZZER ON THESE GUYS.

CHAPTER
FIVE

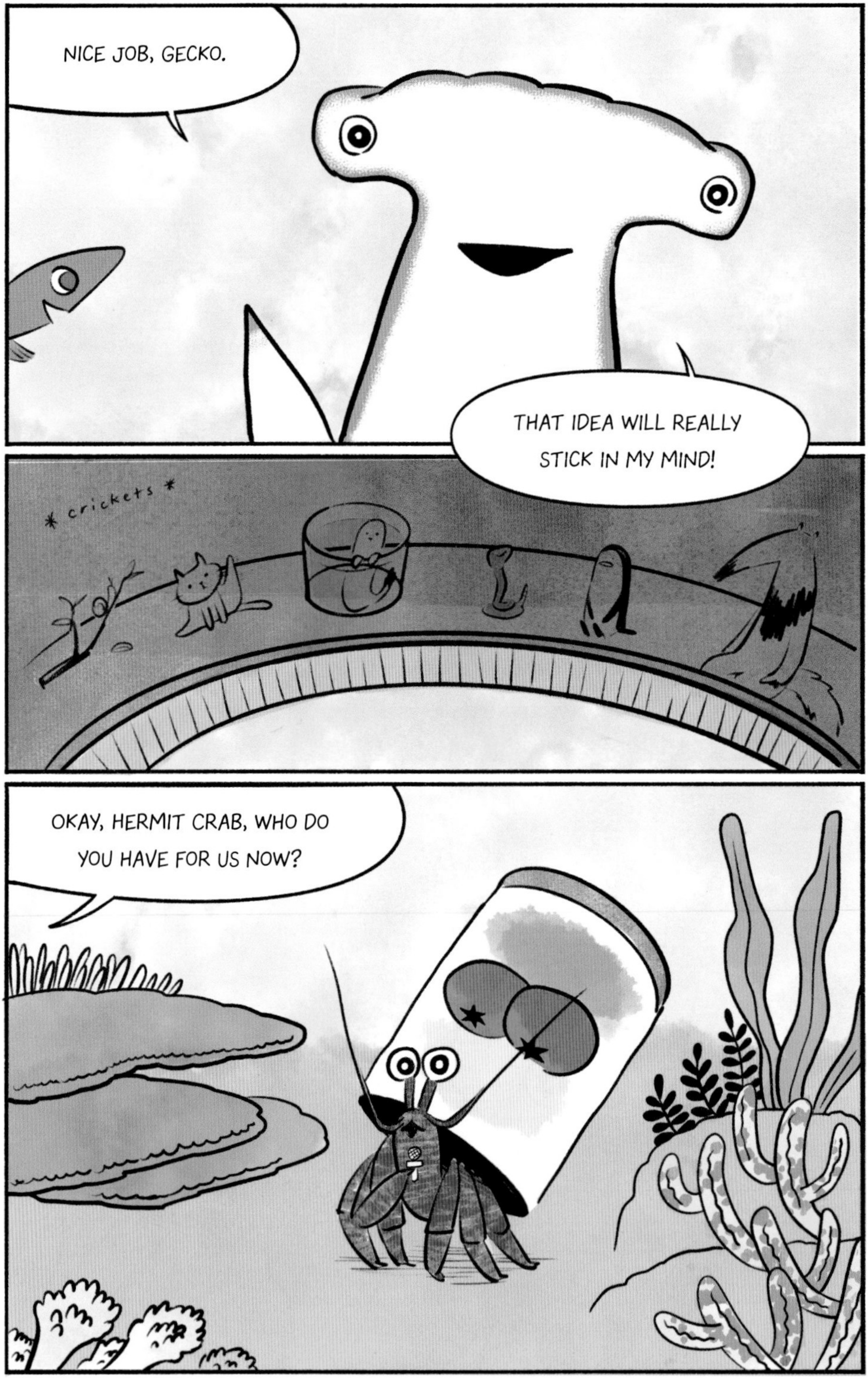
NICE JOB, GECKO.
THAT IDEA WILL REALLY STICK IN MY MIND!
* crickets *
OKAY, HERMIT CRAB, WHO DO YOU HAVE FOR US NOW?

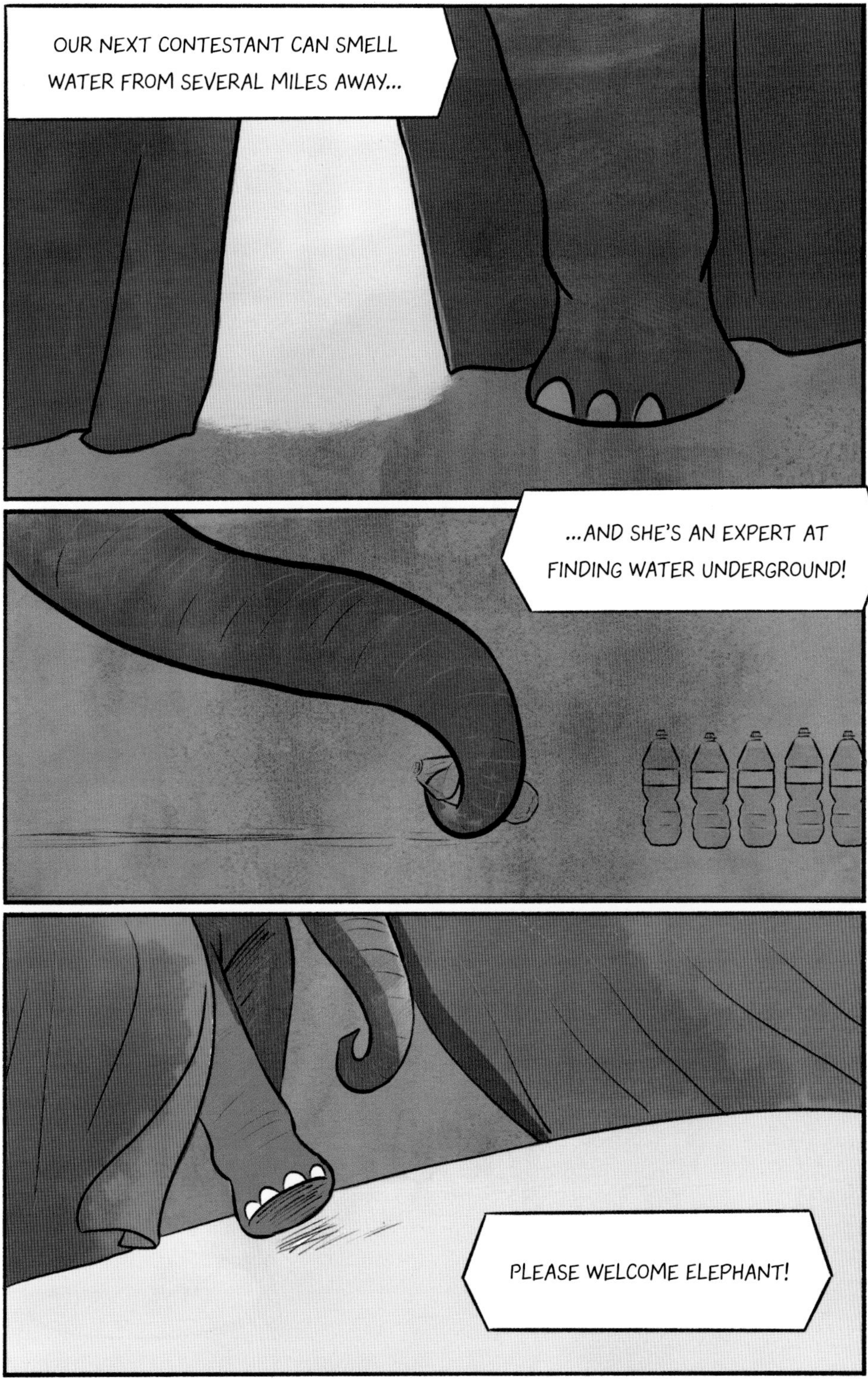
OUR NEXT CONTESTANT CAN SMELL WATER FROM SEVERAL MILES AWAY...
...AND SHE'S AN EXPERT AT FINDING WATER UNDERGROUND!
PLEASE WELCOME ELEPHANT!

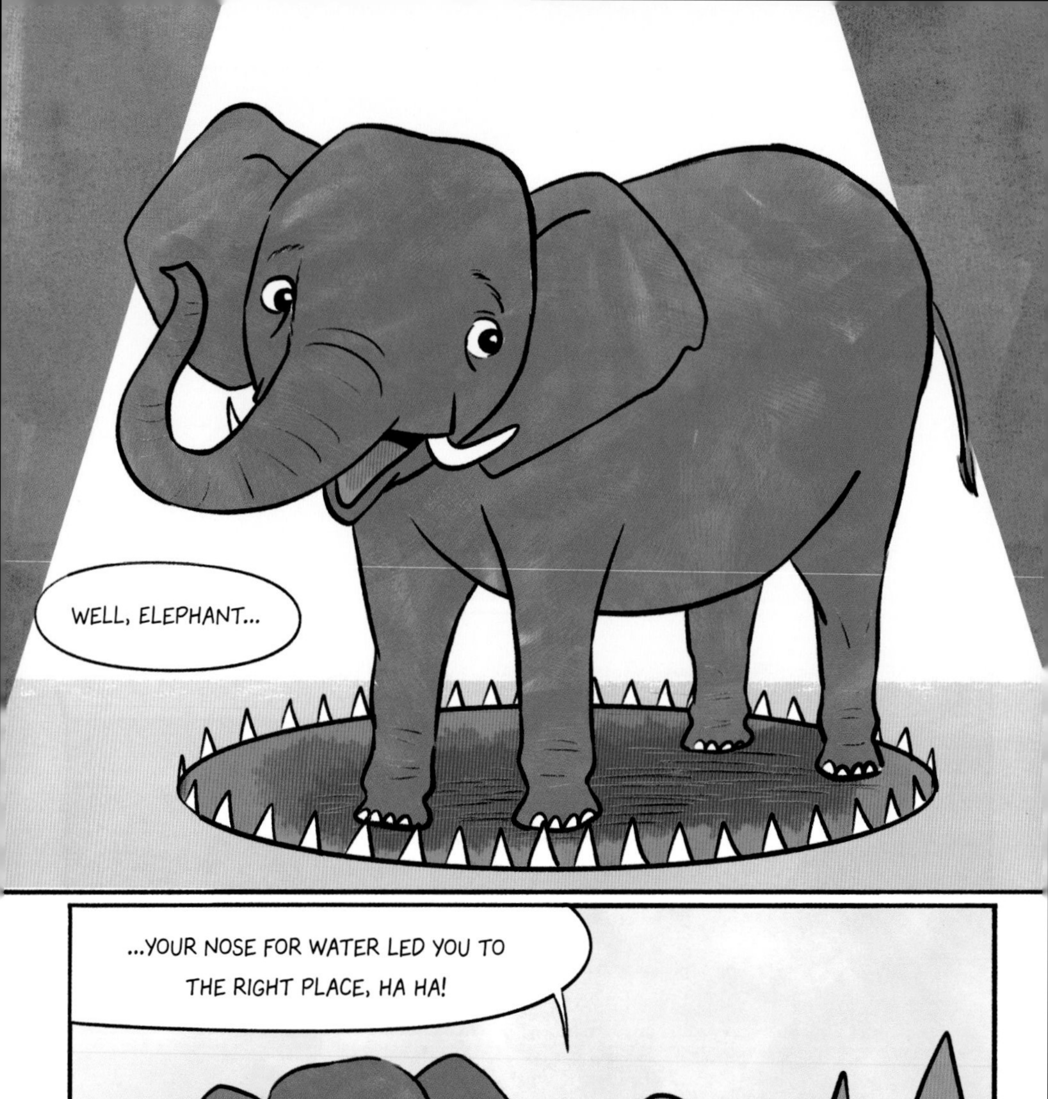
WELL, ELEPHANT...

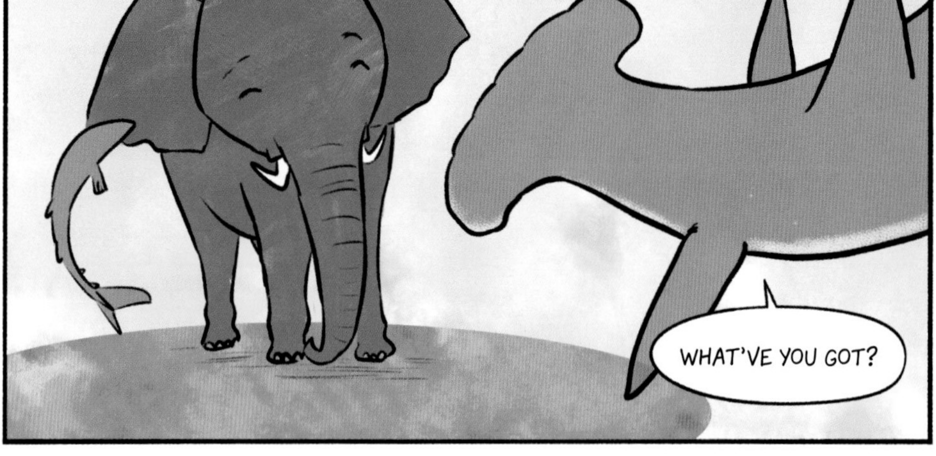
...YOUR NOSE FOR WATER LED YOU TO THE RIGHT PLACE, HA HA!
WHAT'VE YOU GOT?

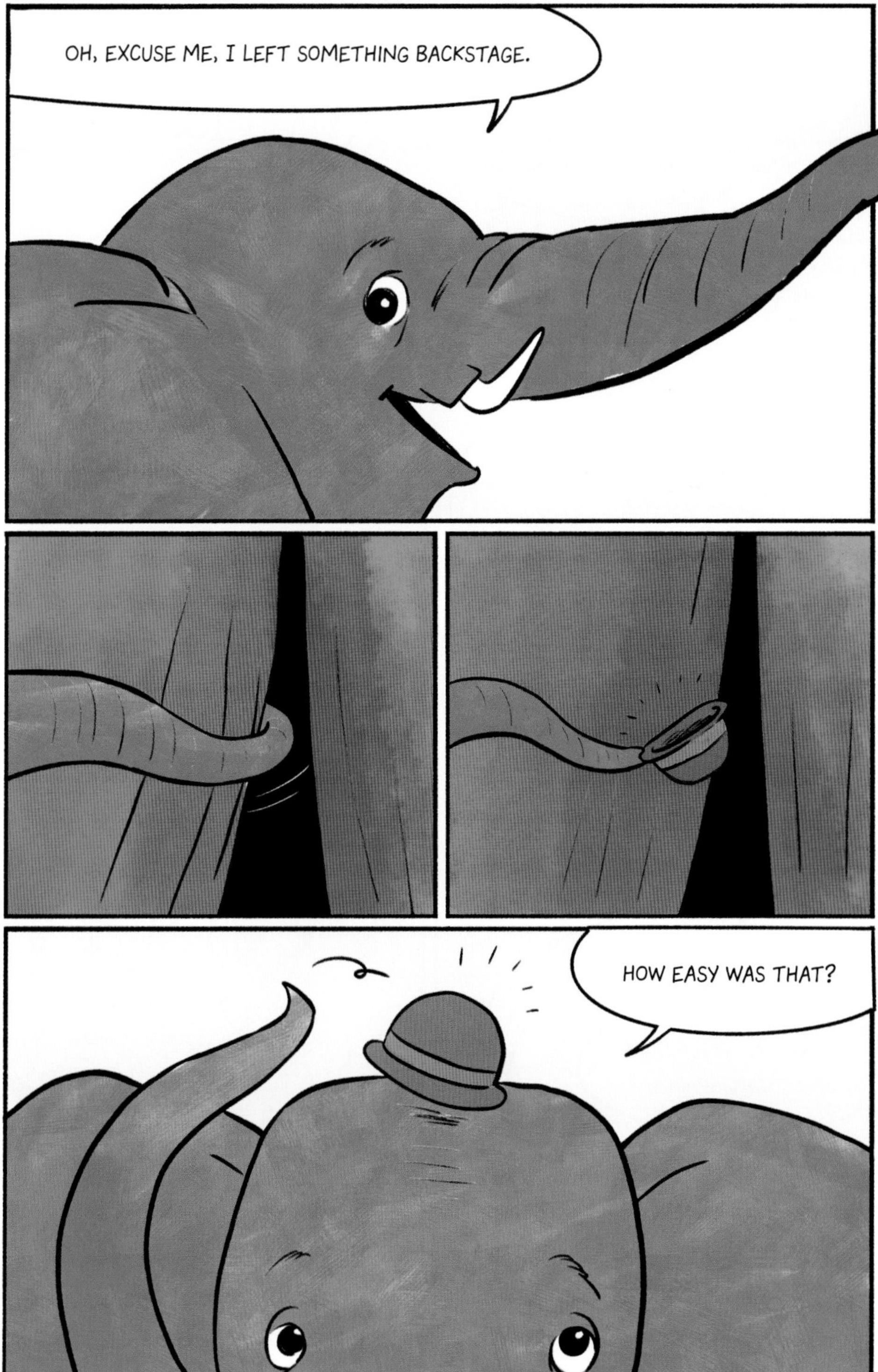
OH, EXCUSE ME, I LEFT SOMETHING BACKSTAGE.
HOW EASY WAS THAT?

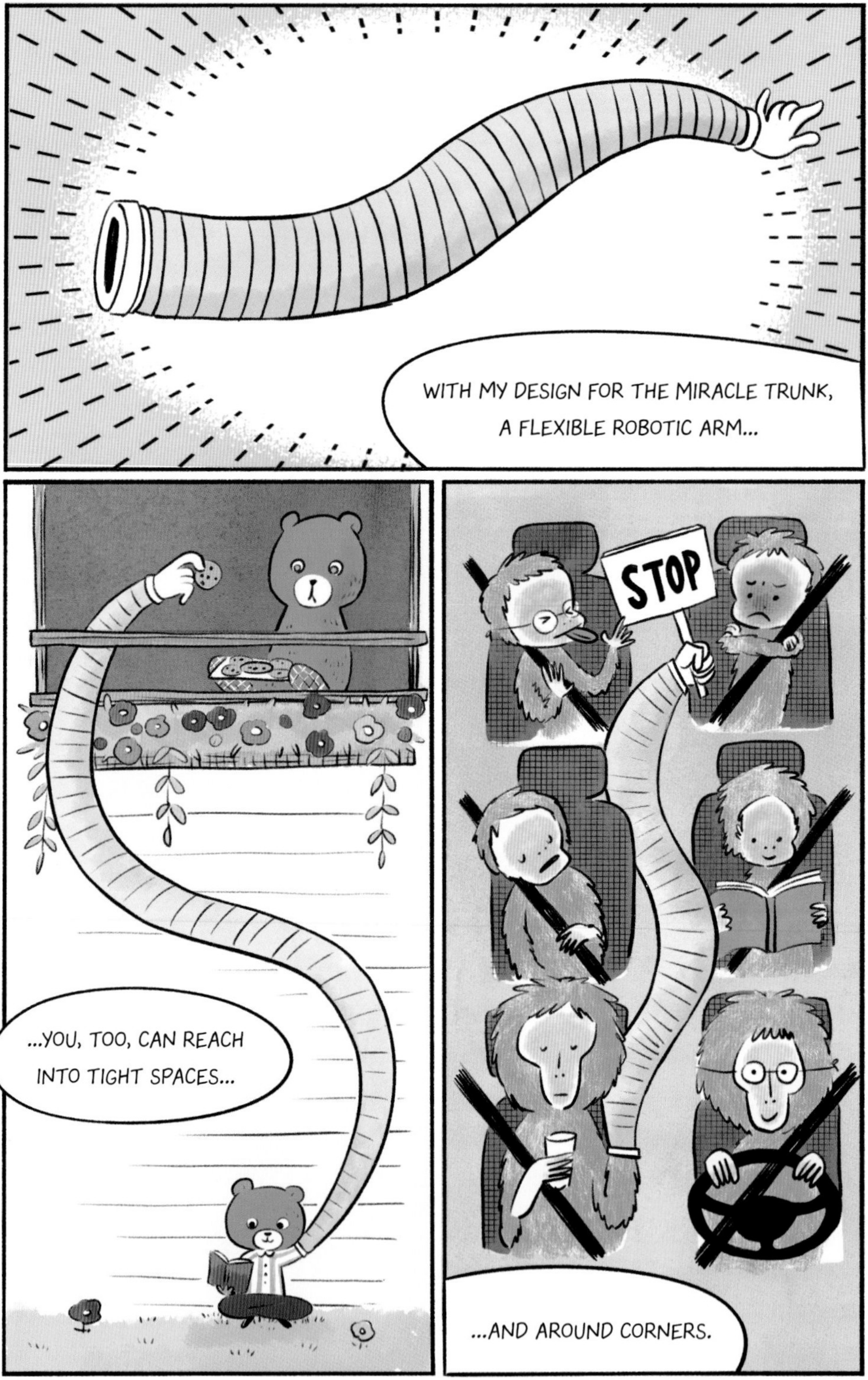
WITH MY DESIGN FOR THE MIRACLE TRUNK, A FLEXIBLE ROBOTIC ARM...
...YOU, TOO, CAN REACH INTO TIGHT SPACES...
STOP
...AND AROUND CORNERS.

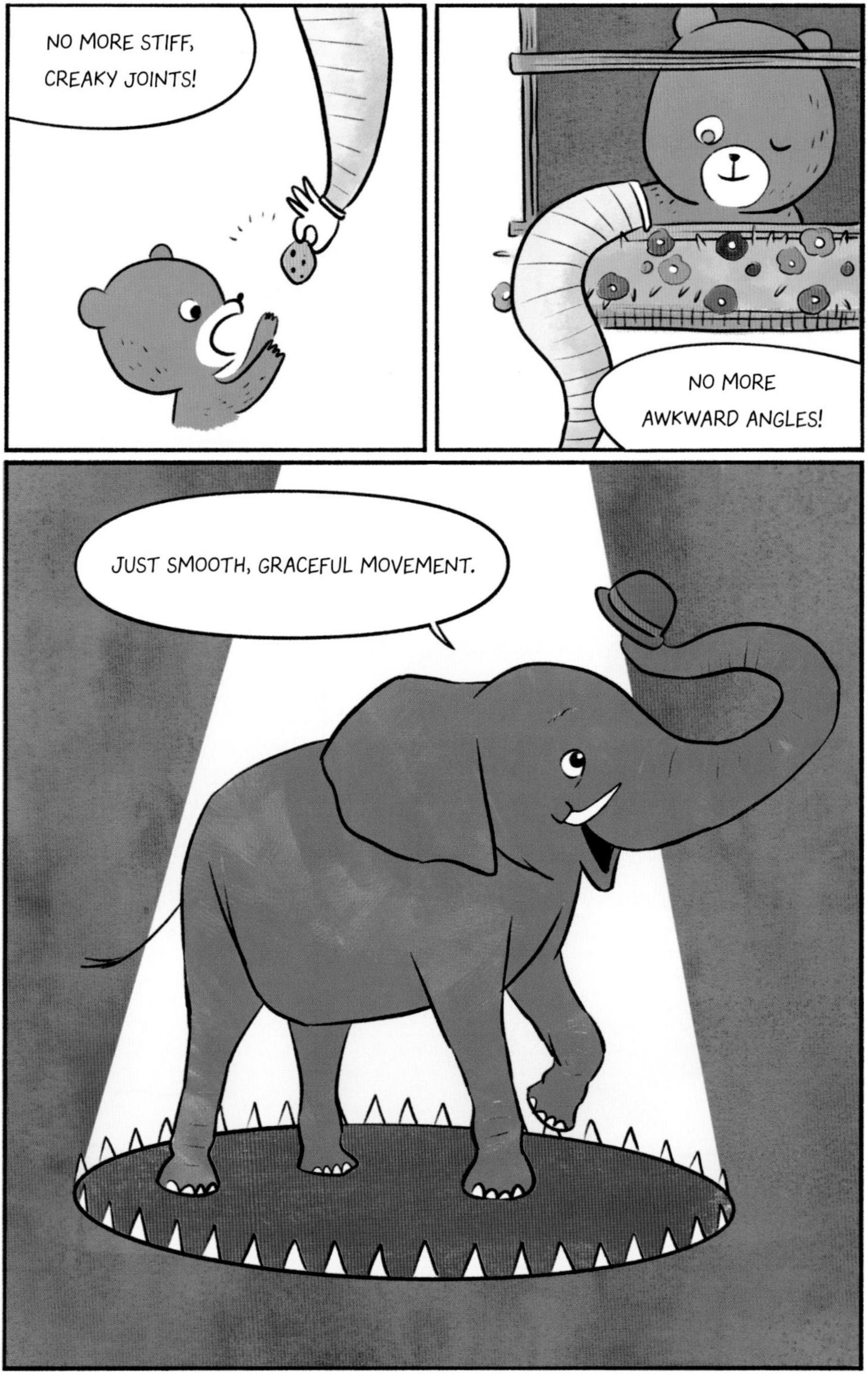
NO MORE STIFF, CREAKY JOINTS!
NO MORE AWKWARD ANGLES!
JUST SMOOTH, GRACEFUL MOVEMENT.

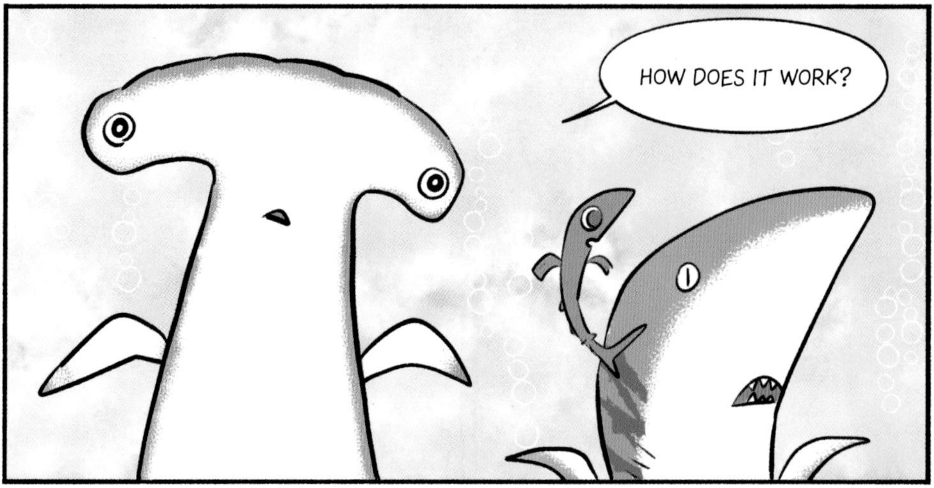
HOW DOES IT WORK?

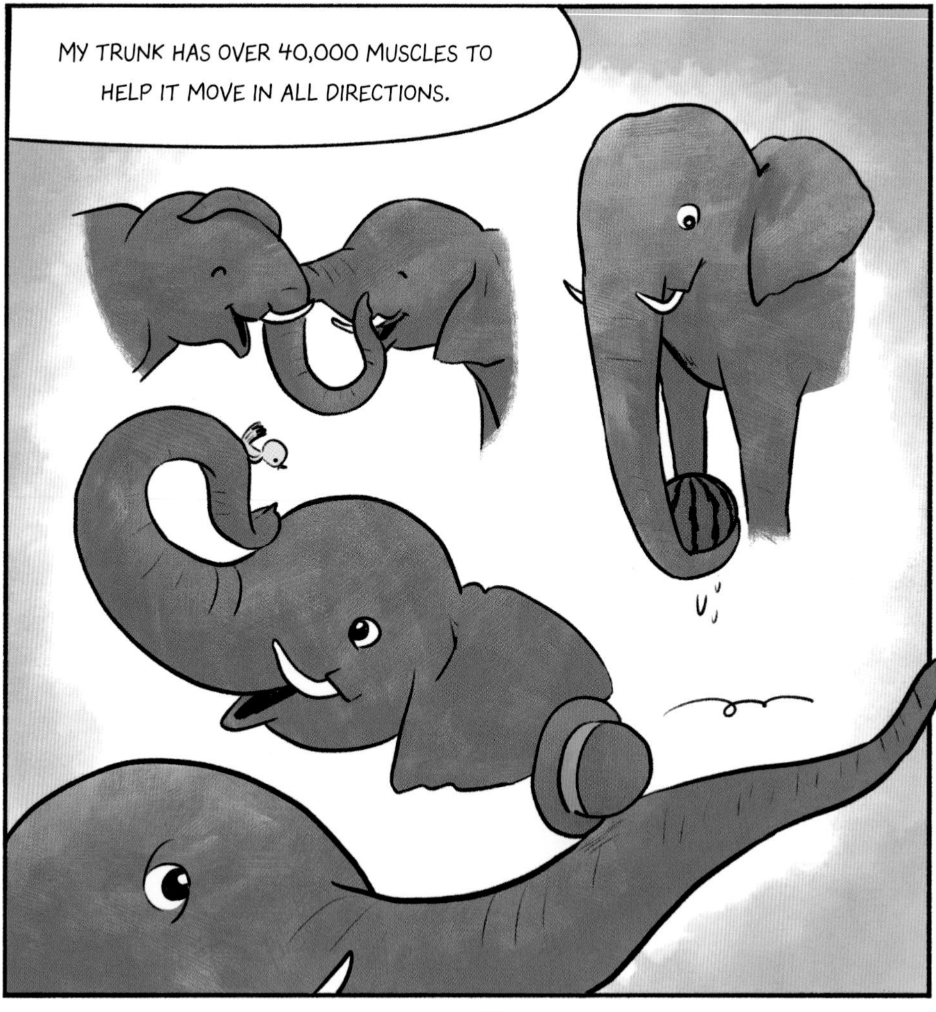
MY TRUNK HAS OVER 40,000 MUSCLES TO HELP IT MOVE IN ALL DIRECTIONS.

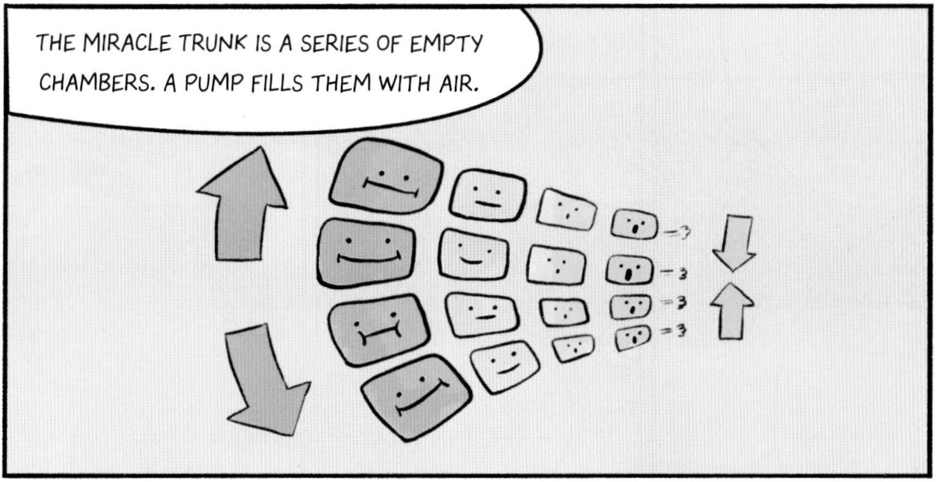
THE MIRACLE TRUNK IS A SERIES OF EMPTY CHAMBERS. A PUMP FILLS THEM WITH AIR.

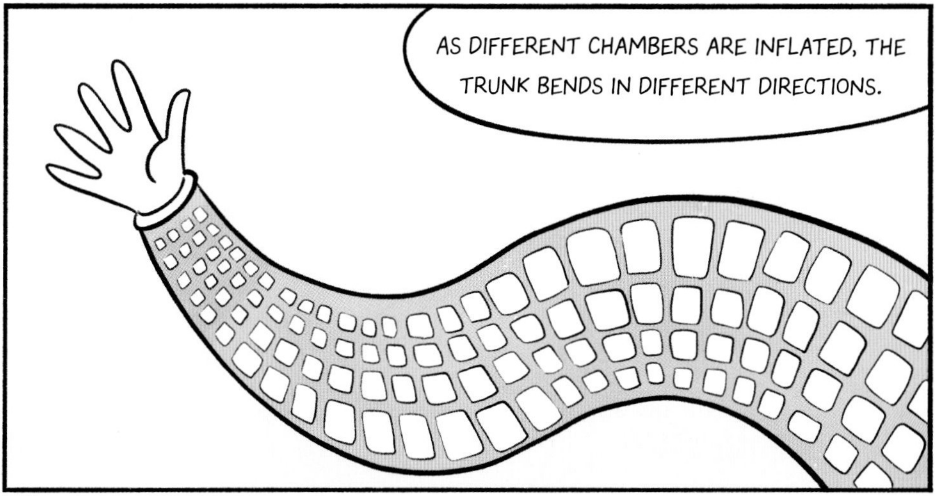
AS DIFFERENT CHAMBERS ARE INFLATED, THE TRUNK BENDS IN DIFFERENT DIRECTIONS.

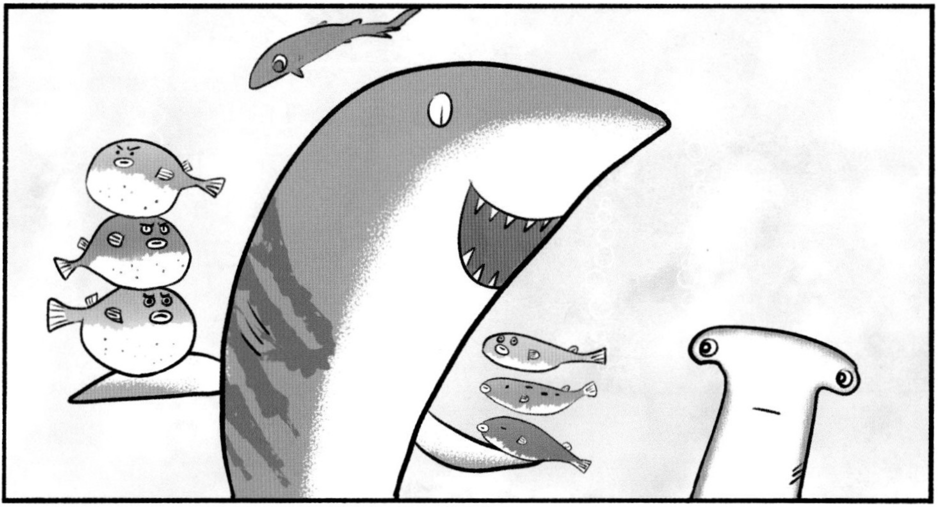

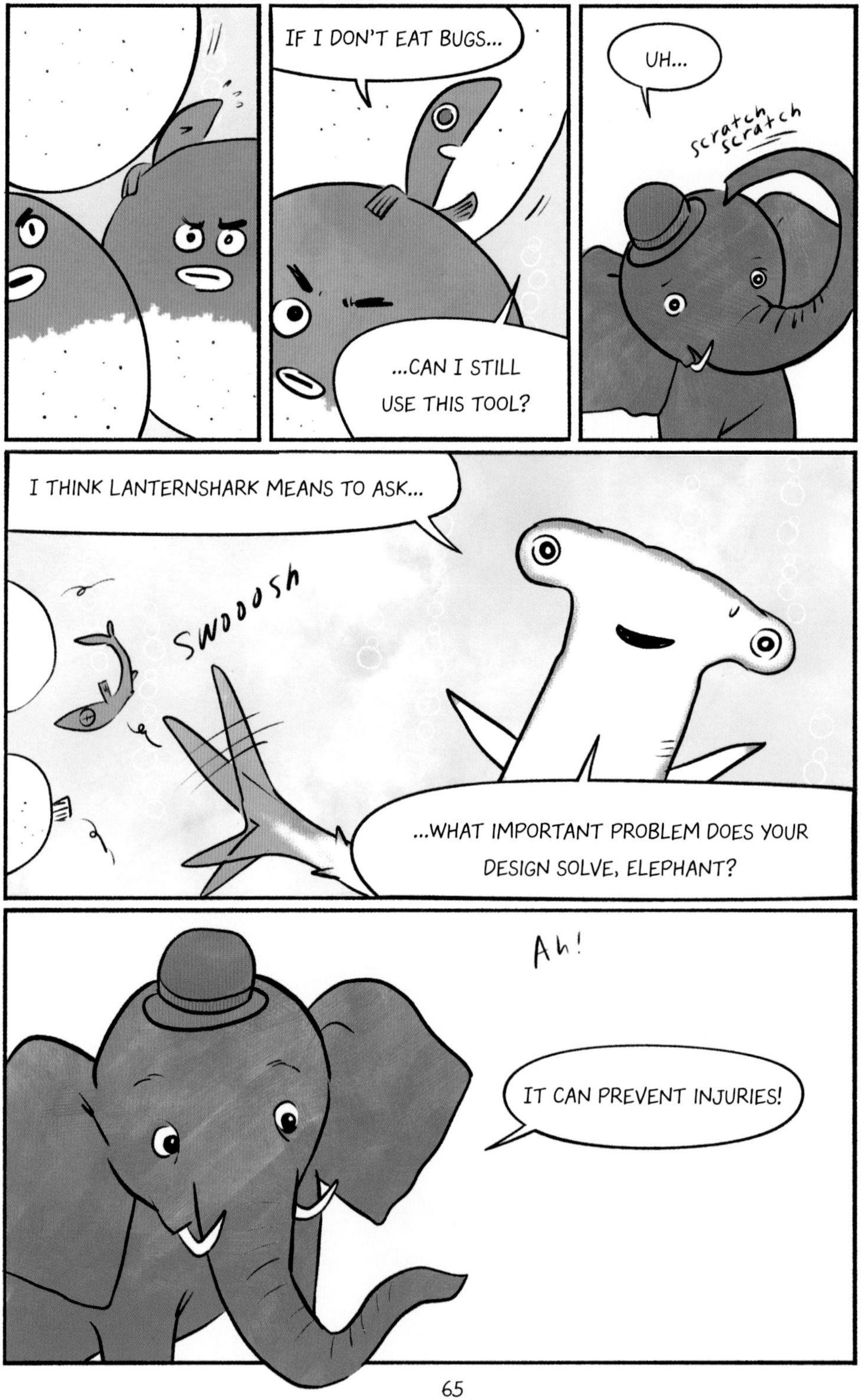
IF I DON'T EAT BUGS...
...CAN I STILL USE THIS TOOL?
UH...
scratch scratch
I THINK LANTERNSHARK MEANS TO ASK...
SWOOOSH
...WHAT IMPORTANT PROBLEM DOES YOUR DESIGN SOLVE, ELEPHANT?
Ah!
IT CAN PREVENT INJURIES!

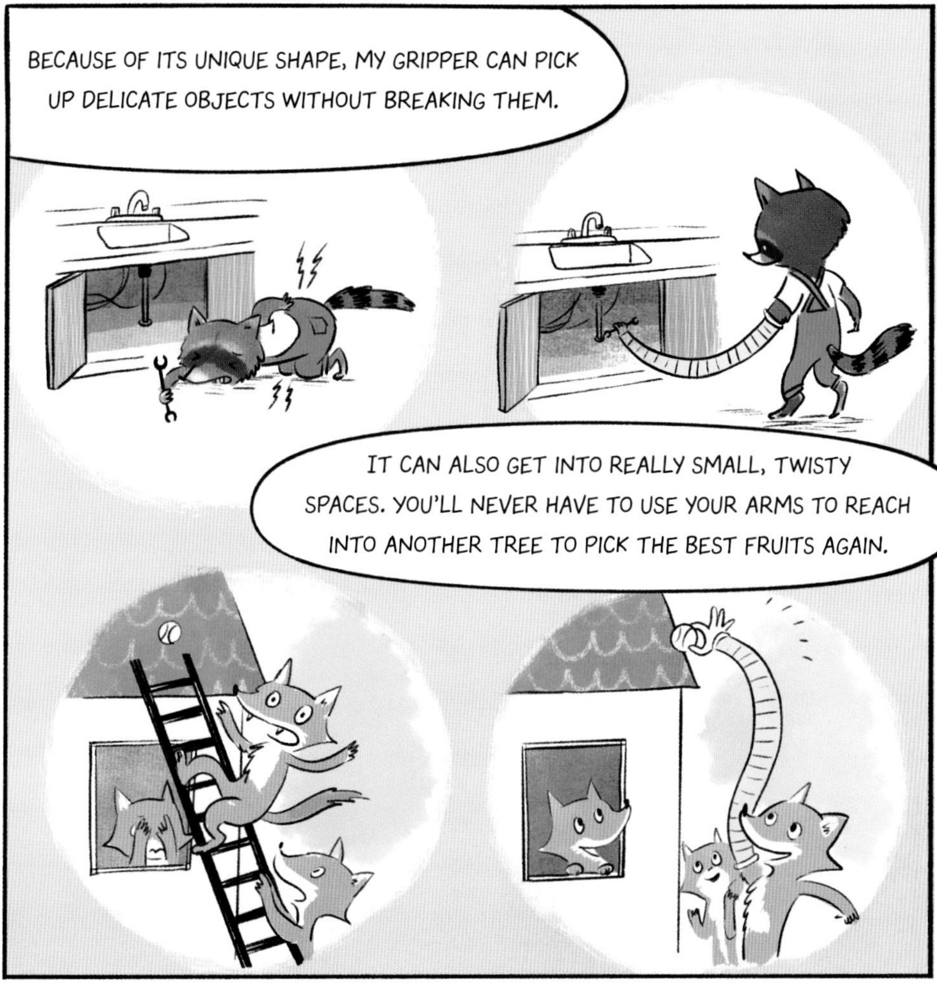
BECAUSE OF ITS UNIQUE SHAPE, MY GRIPPER CAN PICK UP DELICATE OBJECTS WITHOUT BREAKING THEM.
IT CAN ALSO GET INTO REALLY SMALL, TWISTY SPACES. YOU'LL NEVER HAVE TO USE YOUR ARMS TO REACH INTO ANOTHER TREE TO PICK THE BEST FRUITS AGAIN.

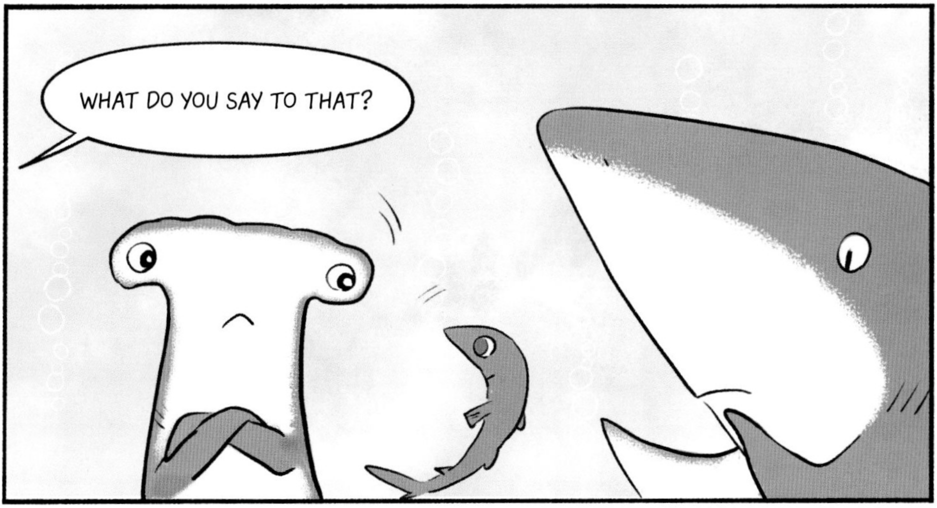
WHAT DO YOU SAY TO THAT?

CHAPTER
SIX

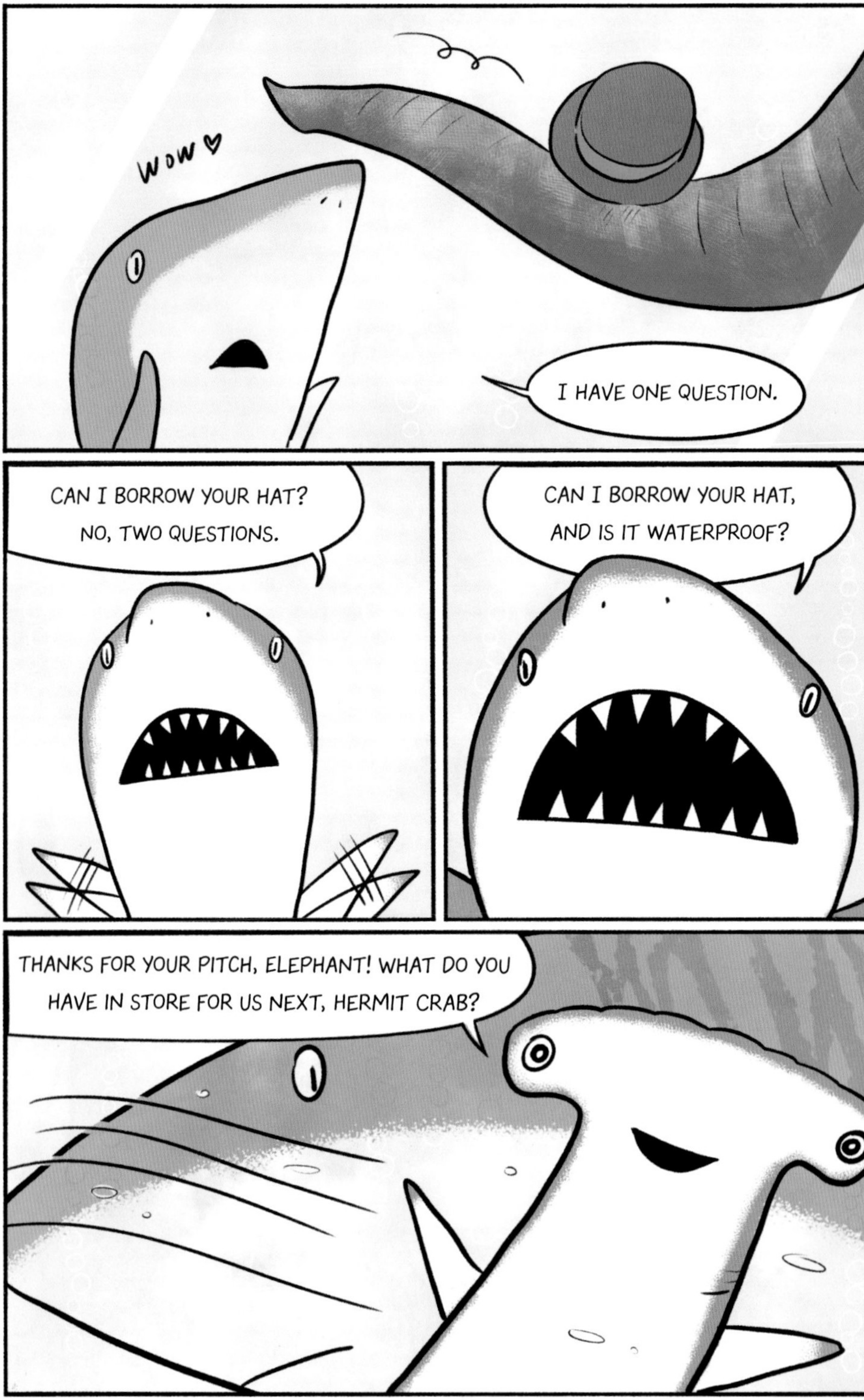
WOW ♡
I HAVE ONE QUESTION.
CAN I BORROW YOUR HAT? NO, TWO QUESTIONS.
CAN I BORROW YOUR HAT, AND IS IT WATERPROOF?
THANKS FOR YOUR PITCH, ELEPHANT! WHAT DO YOU HAVE IN STORE FOR US NEXT, HERMIT CRAB?

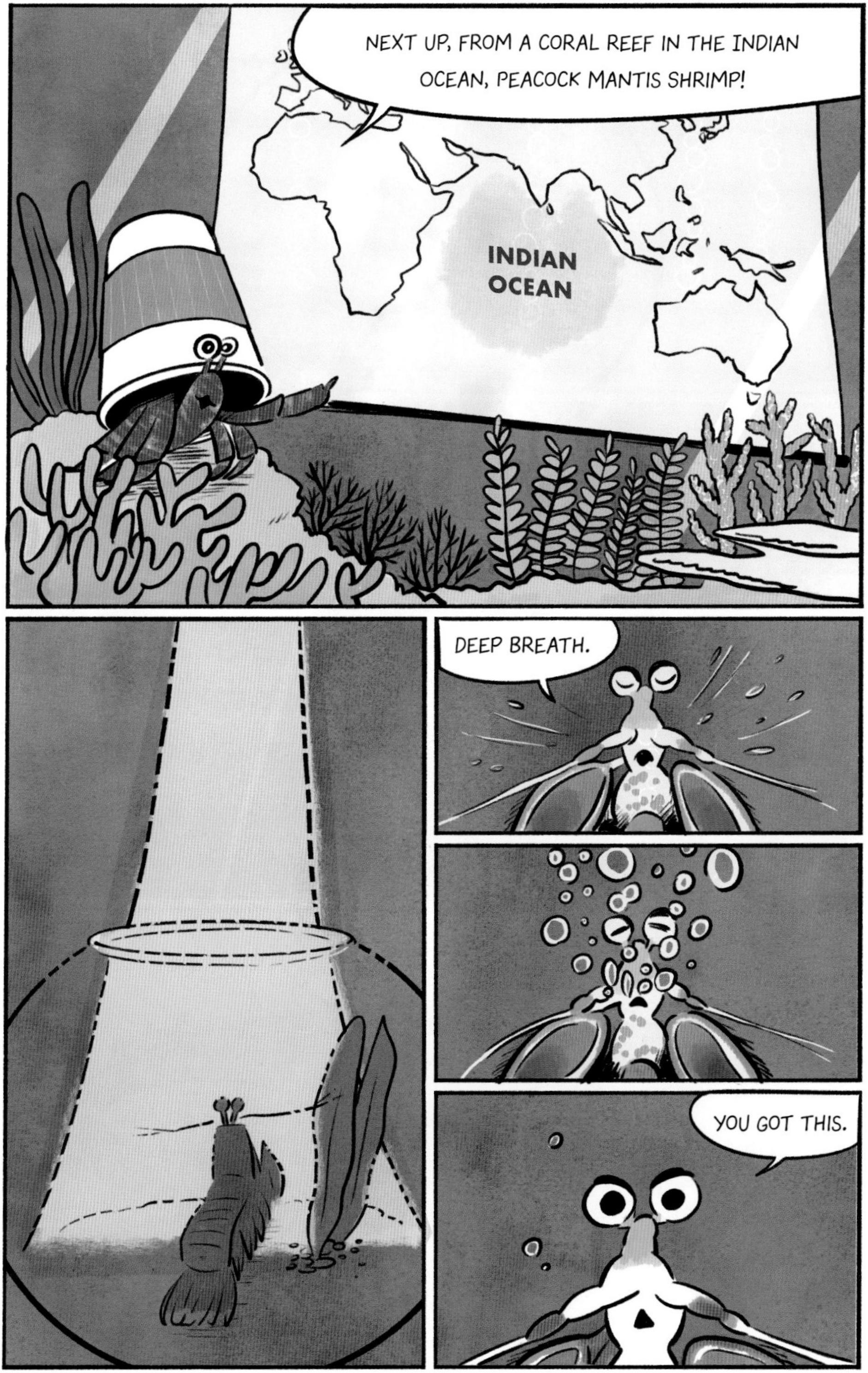
NEXT UP, FROM A CORAL REEF IN THE INDIAN OCEAN, PEACOCK MANTIS SHRIMP!
INDIAN OCEAN
DEEP BREATH.
YOU GOT THIS.

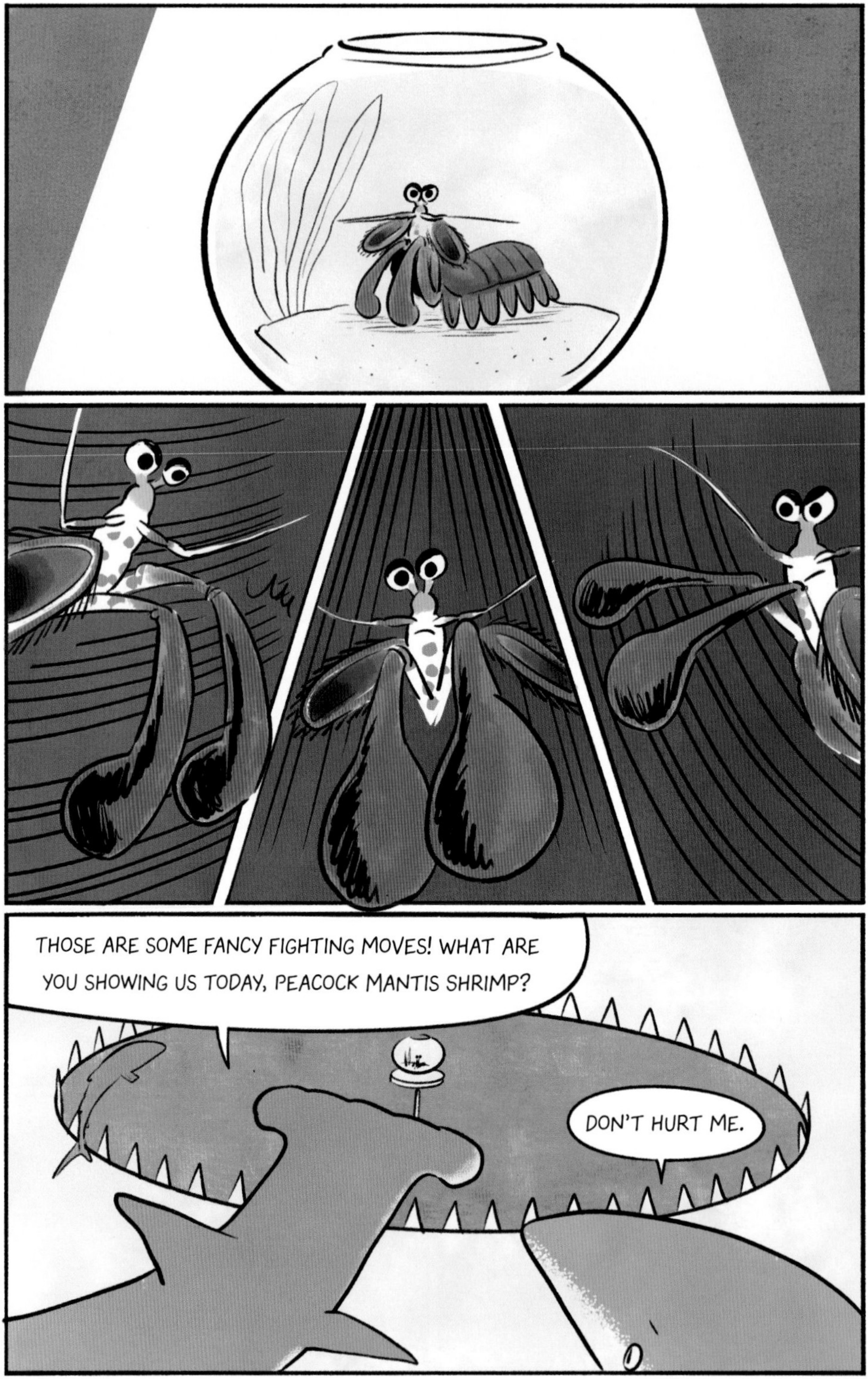
THOSE ARE SOME FANCY FIGHTING MOVES! WHAT ARE YOU SHOWING US TODAY, PEACOCK MANTIS SHRIMP?
DON'T HURT ME.

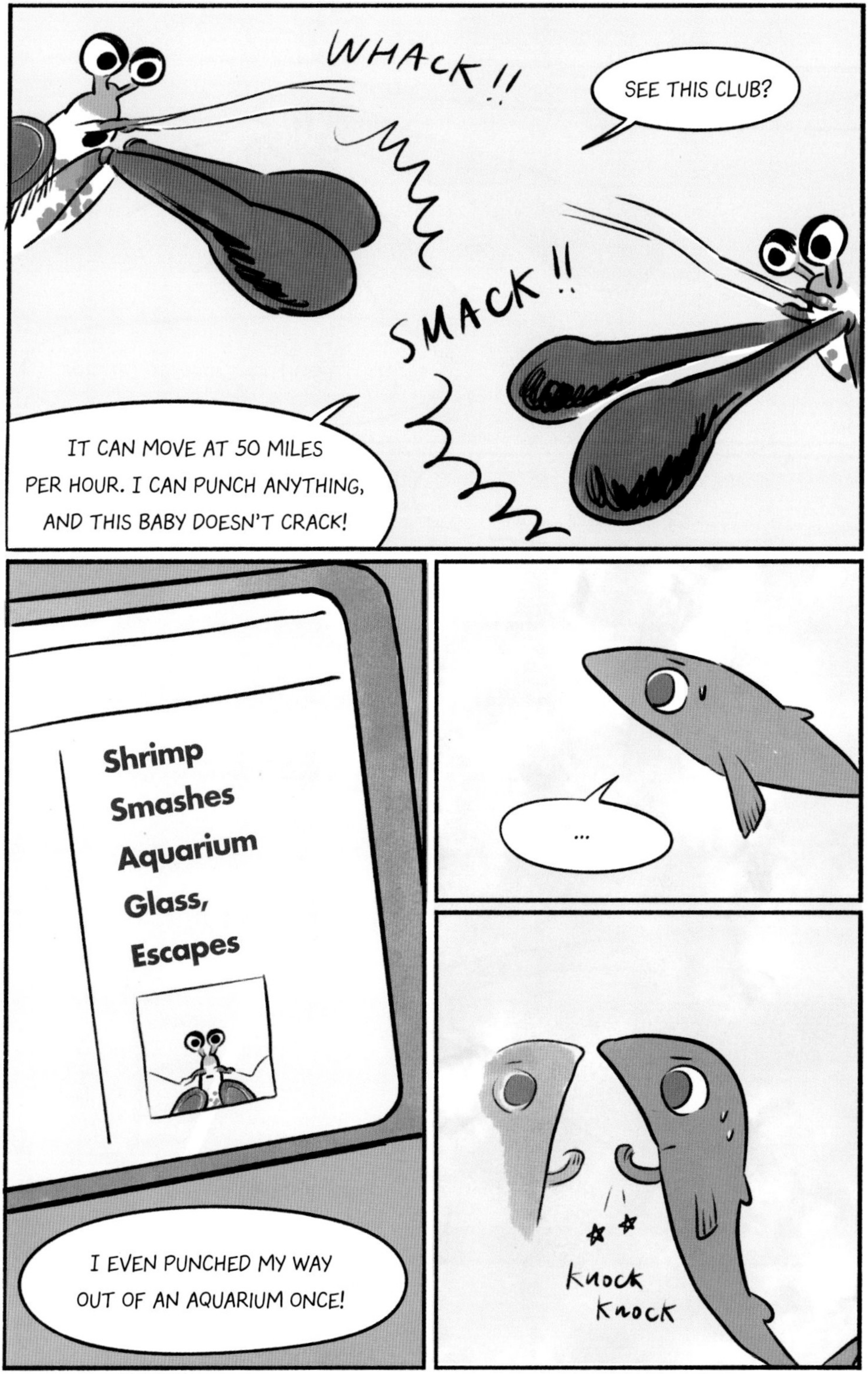
WHACK!!
SEE THIS CLUB?
SMACK!!
IT CAN MOVE AT 50 MILES PER HOUR. I CAN PUNCH ANYTHING, AND THIS BABY DOESN'T CRACK!
Shrimp Smashes Aquarium Glass, Escapes
I EVEN PUNCHED MY WAY OUT OF AN AQUARIUM ONCE!
...
knock knock

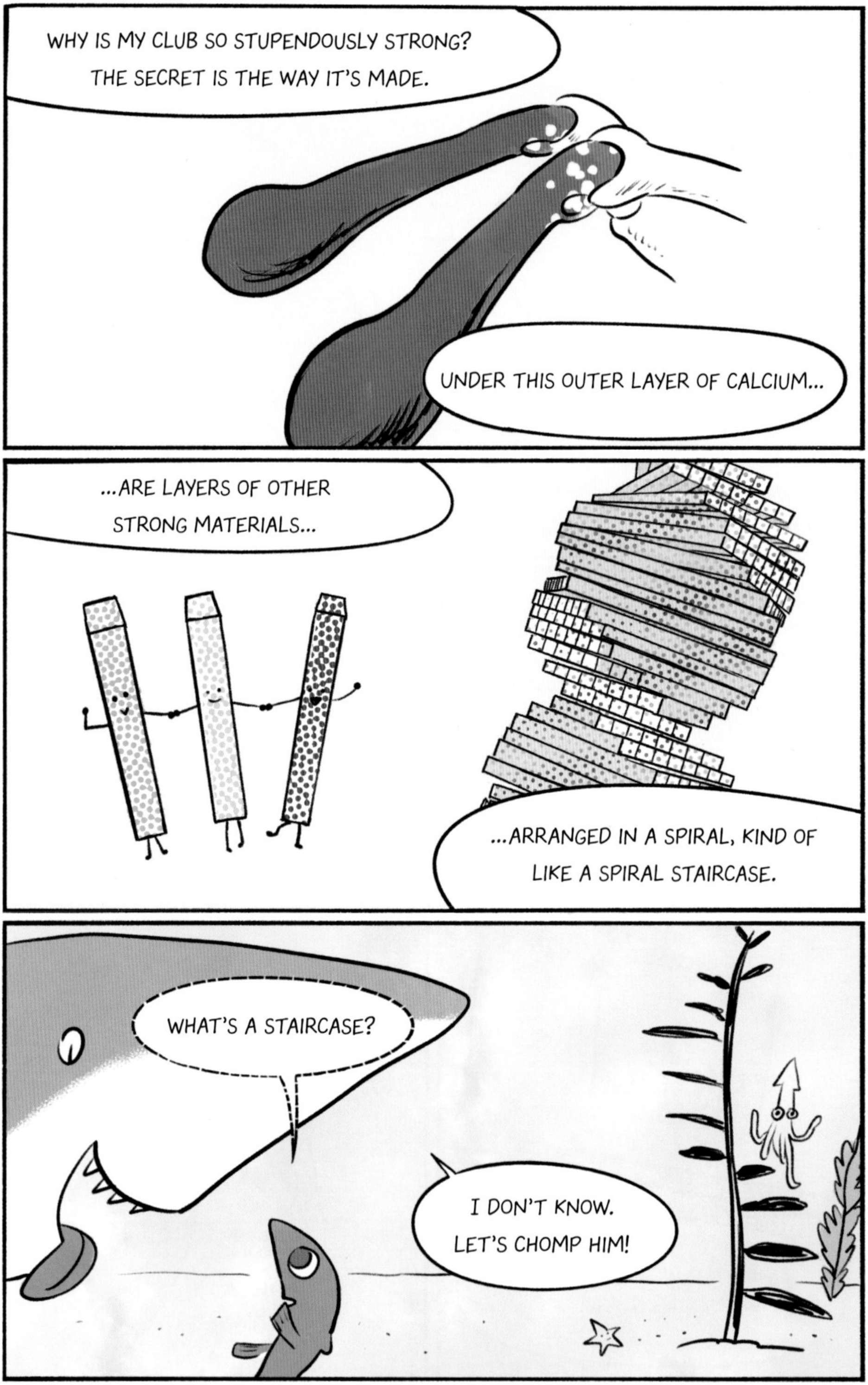
WHY IS MY CLUB SO STUPENDOUSLY STRONG? THE SECRET IS THE WAY IT'S MADE.
UNDER THIS OUTER LAYER OF CALCIUM...
...ARE LAYERS OF OTHER STRONG MATERIALS...
...ARRANGED IN A SPIRAL, KIND OF LIKE A SPIRAL STAIRCASE.
WHAT'S A STAIRCASE?
I DON'T KNOW. LET'S CHOMP HIM!

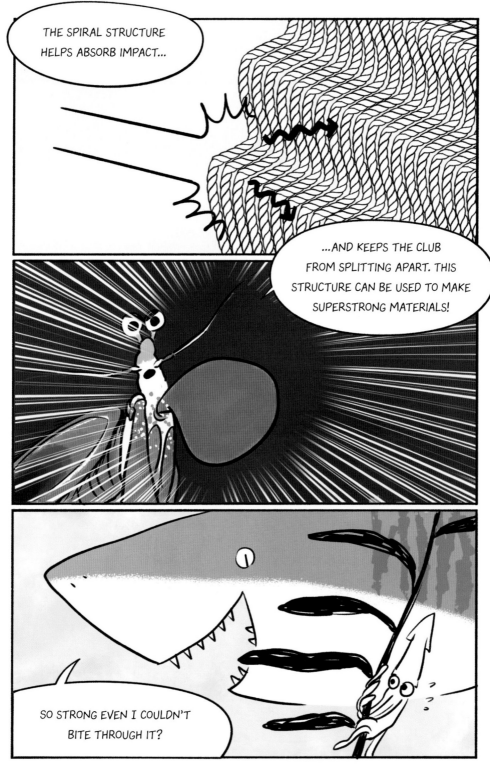

THE SPIRAL STRUCTURE HELPS ABSORB IMPACT...

...AND KEEPS THE CLUB FROM SPLITTING APART. THIS STRUCTURE CAN BE USED TO MAKE SUPERSTRONG MATERIALS!

SO STRONG EVEN I COULDN'T BITE THROUGH IT?

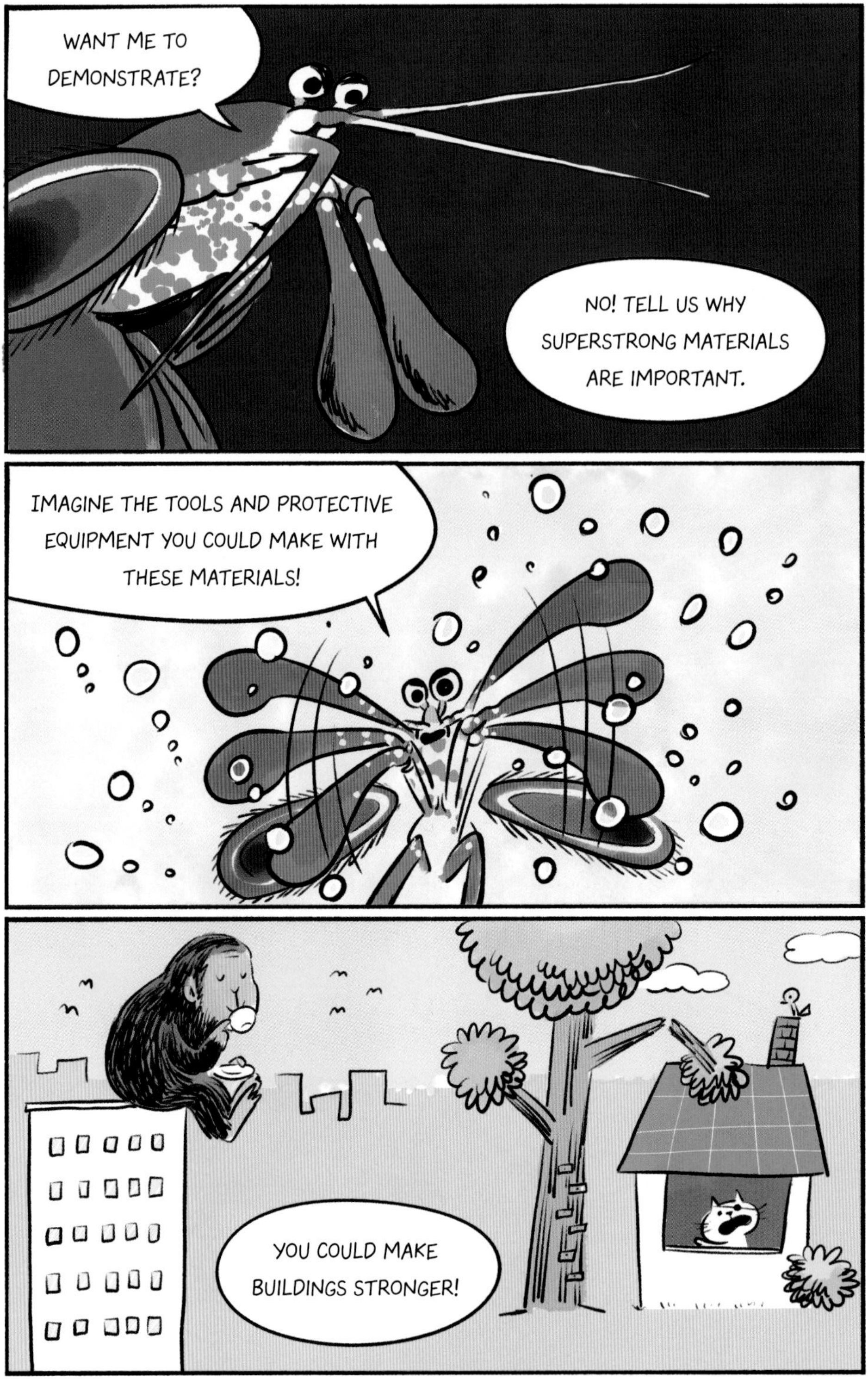
WANT ME TO DEMONSTRATE?
NO! TELL US WHY SUPERSTRONG MATERIALS ARE IMPORTANT.
IMAGINE THE TOOLS AND PROTECTIVE EQUIPMENT YOU COULD MAKE WITH THESE MATERIALS!
YOU COULD MAKE BUILDINGS STRONGER!

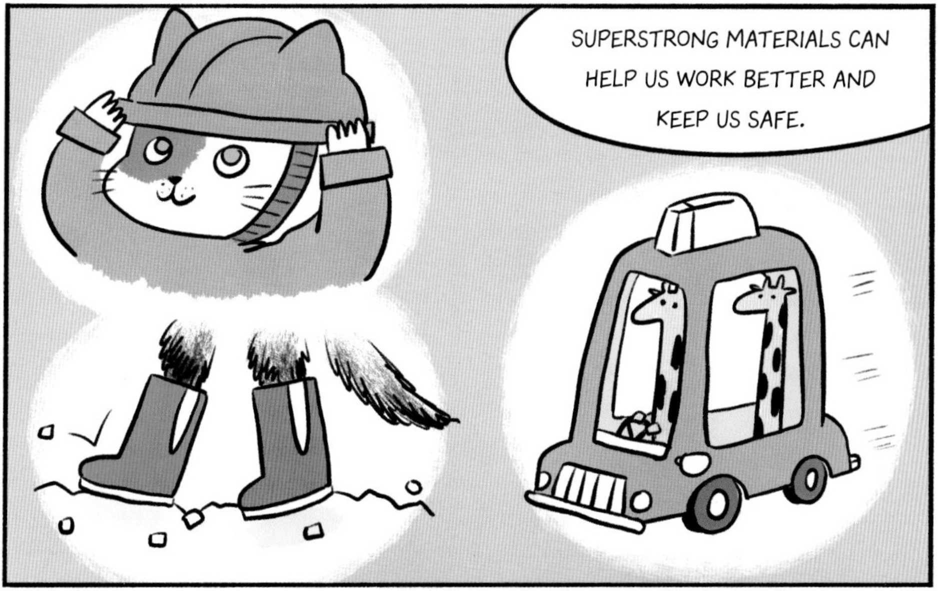
SUPERSTRONG MATERIALS CAN HELP US WORK BETTER AND KEEP US SAFE.

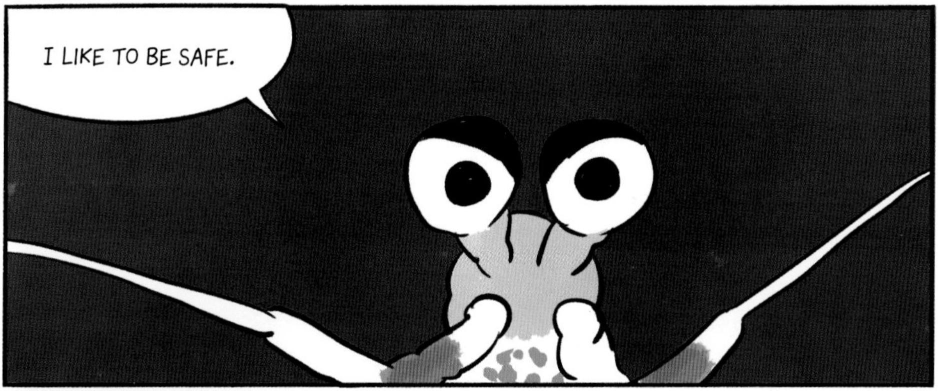
I LIKE TO BE SAFE.

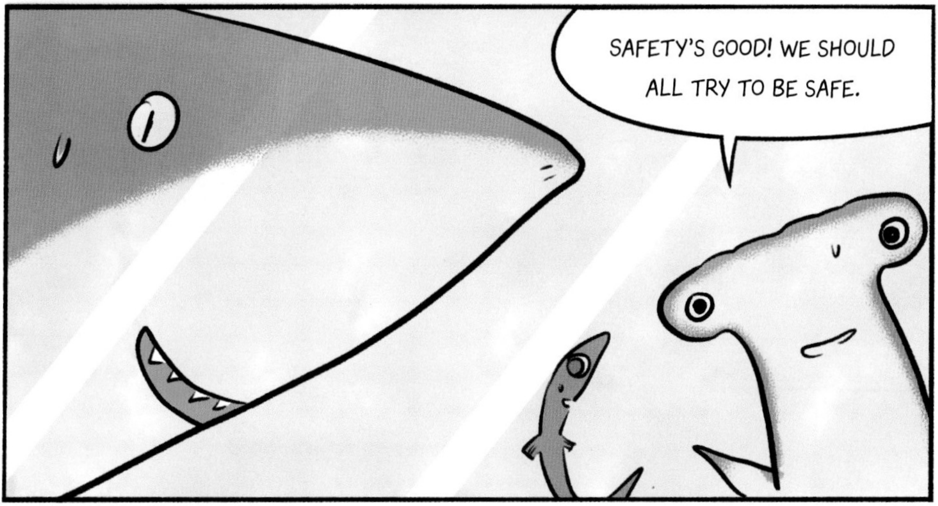
SAFETY'S GOOD! WE SHOULD ALL TRY TO BE SAFE.

CHAPTER SEVEN

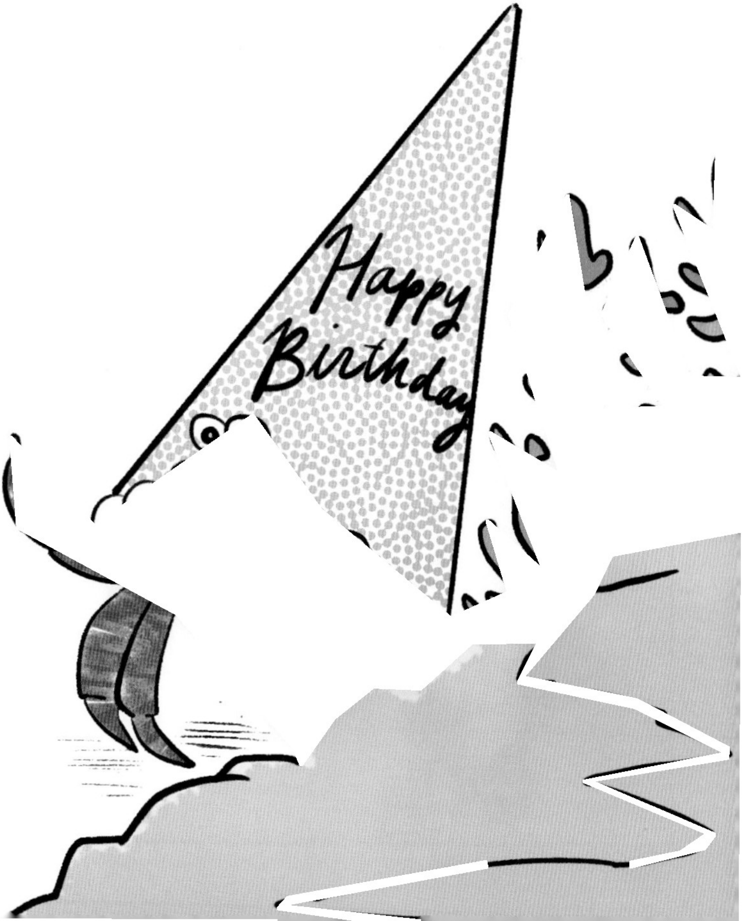
Happy Birthday

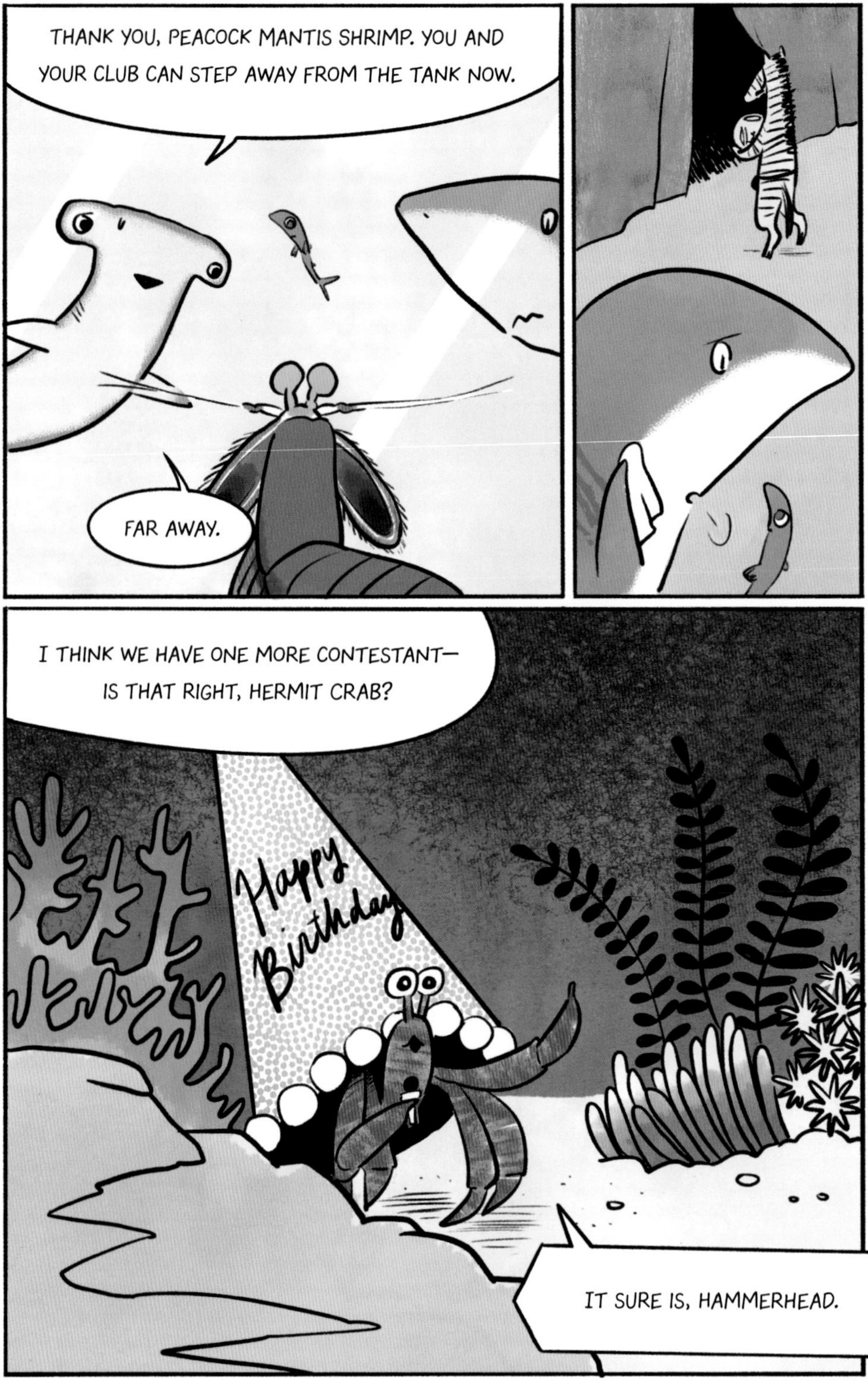
THANK YOU, PEACOCK MANTIS SHRIMP. YOU AND YOUR CLUB CAN STEP AWAY FROM THE TANK NOW.
FAR AWAY.
I THINK WE HAVE ONE MORE CONTESTANT—IS THAT RIGHT, HERMIT CRAB?
Happy Birthday
IT SURE IS, HAMMERHEAD.

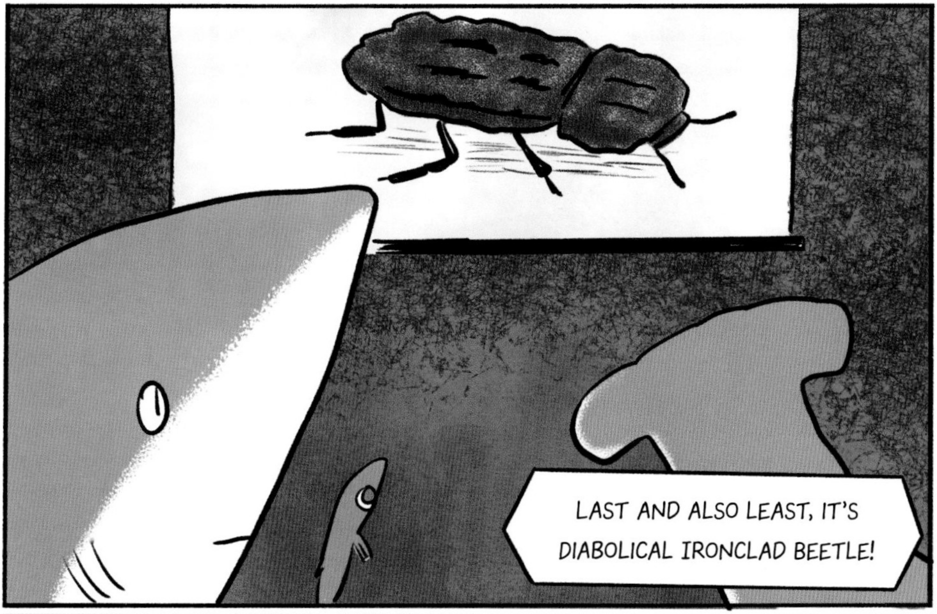
LAST AND ALSO LEAST, IT'S DIABOLICAL IRONCLAD BEETLE!

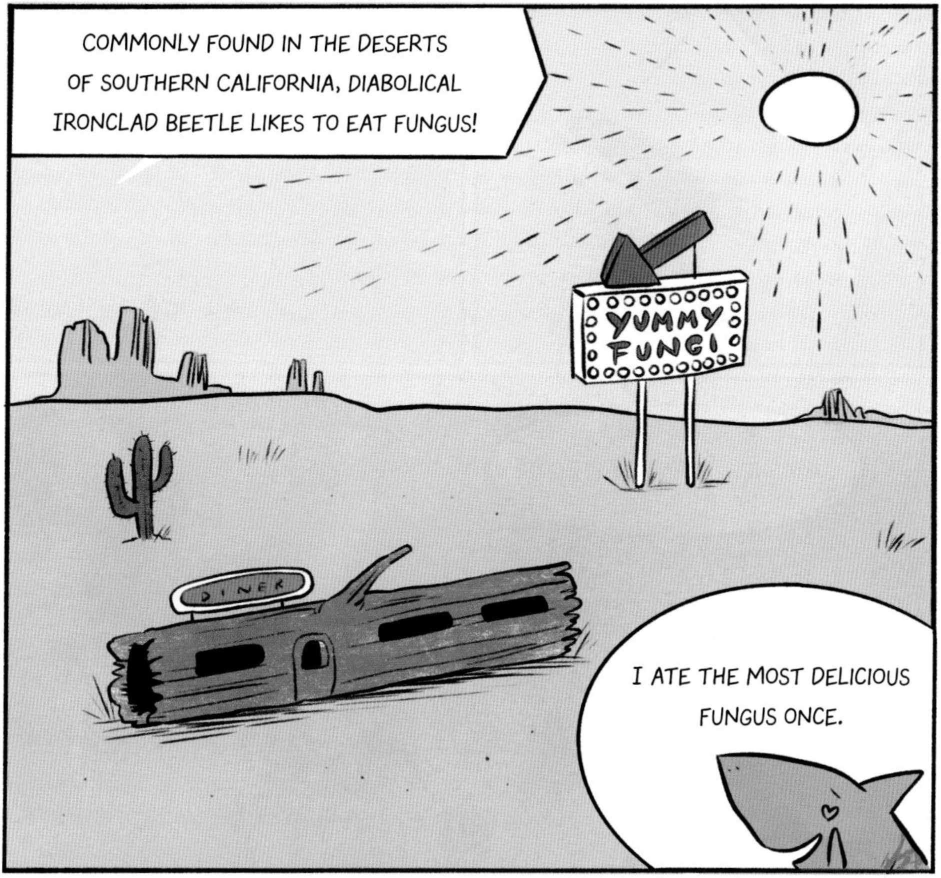
COMMONLY FOUND IN THE DESERTS OF SOUTHERN CALIFORNIA, DIABOLICAL IRONCLAD BEETLE LIKES TO EAT FUNGUS!
YUMMY FUNGI
DINER
I ATE THE MOST DELICIOUS FUNGUS ONCE.

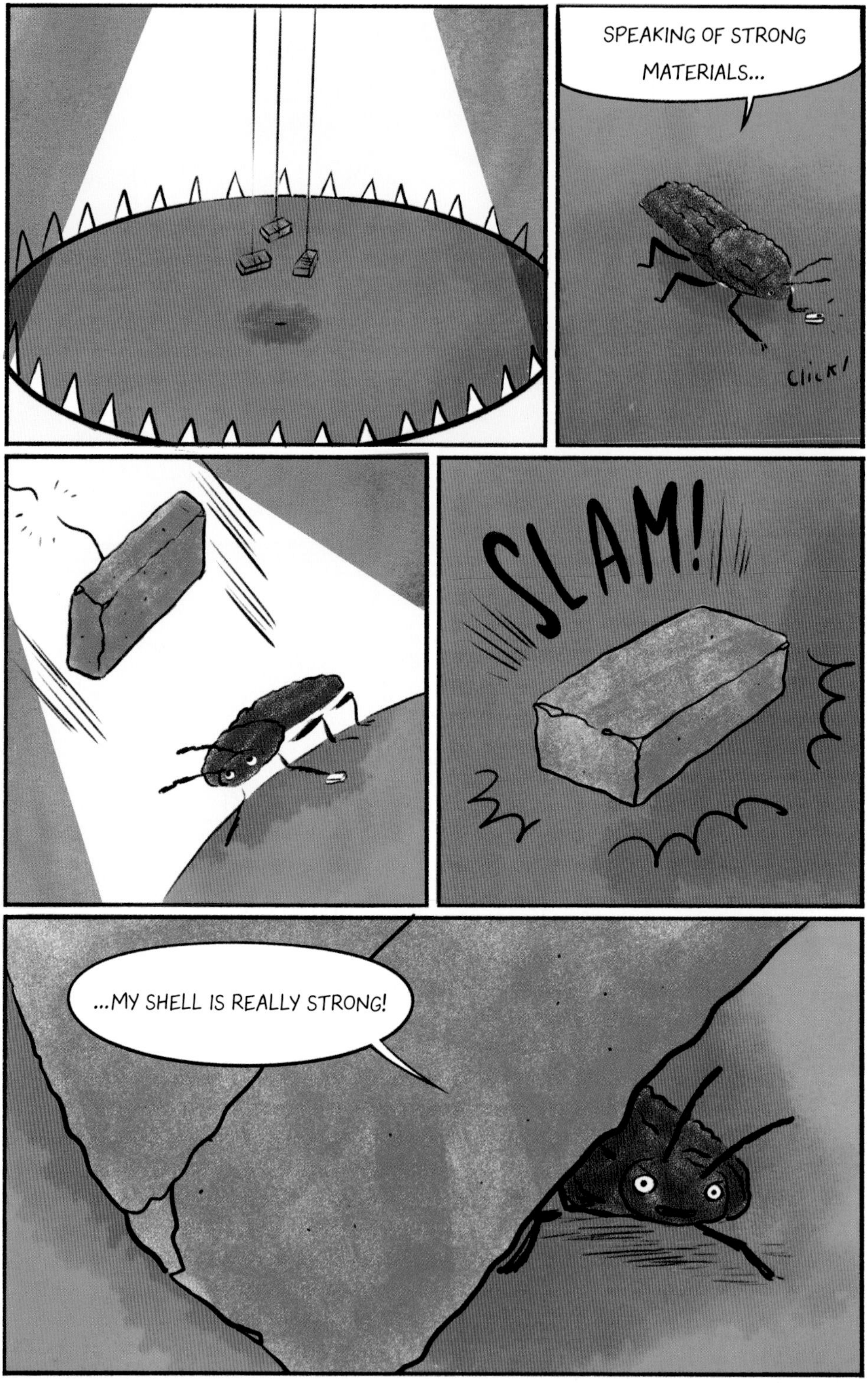
SPEAKING OF STRONG MATERIALS...
CLICK!
SLAM!
...MY SHELL IS REALLY STRONG!

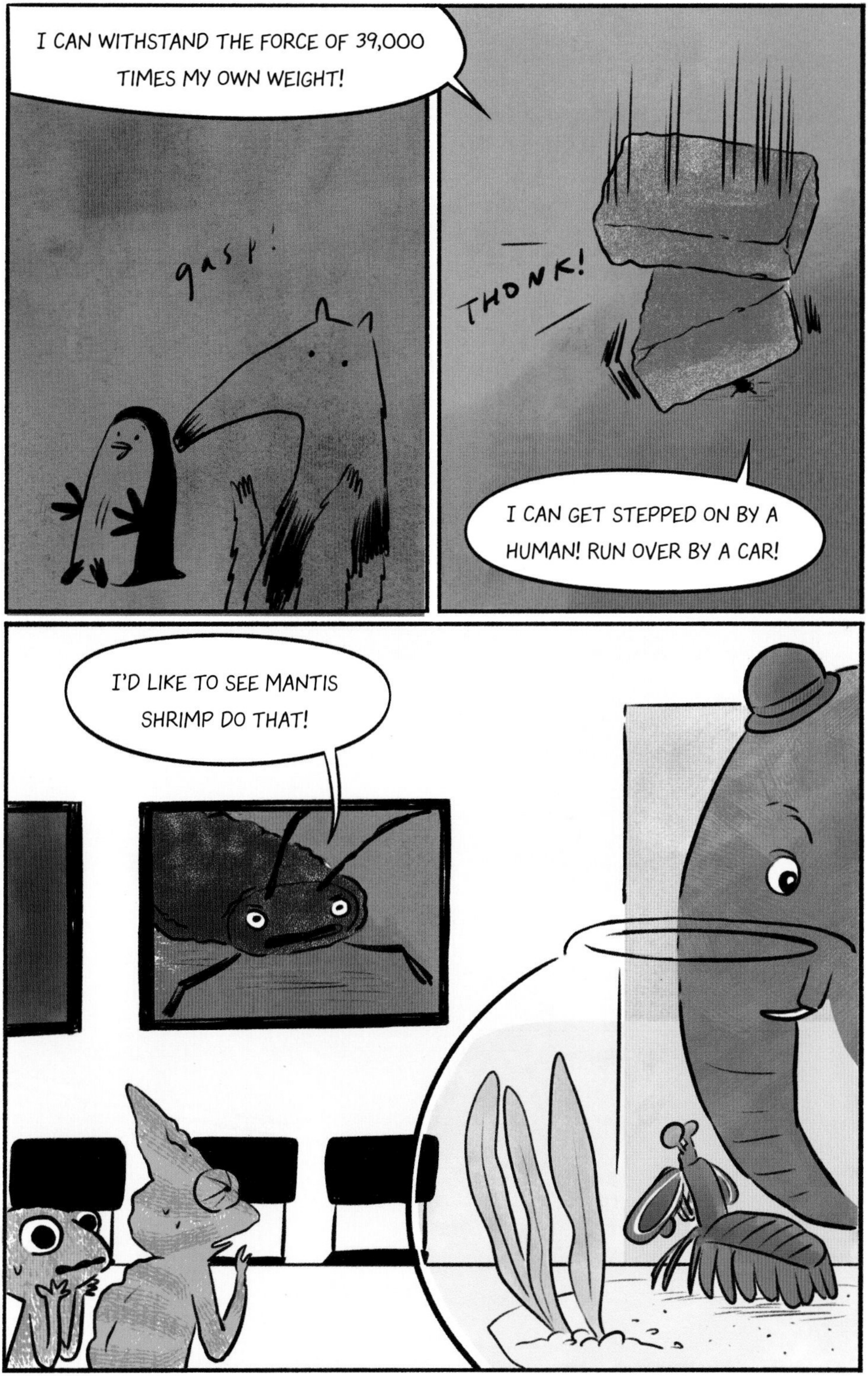
I CAN WITHSTAND THE FORCE OF 39,000 TIMES MY OWN WEIGHT!
gasp!
THONK!
I CAN GET STEPPED ON BY A HUMAN! RUN OVER BY A CAR!
I'D LIKE TO SEE MANTIS SHRIMP DO THAT!

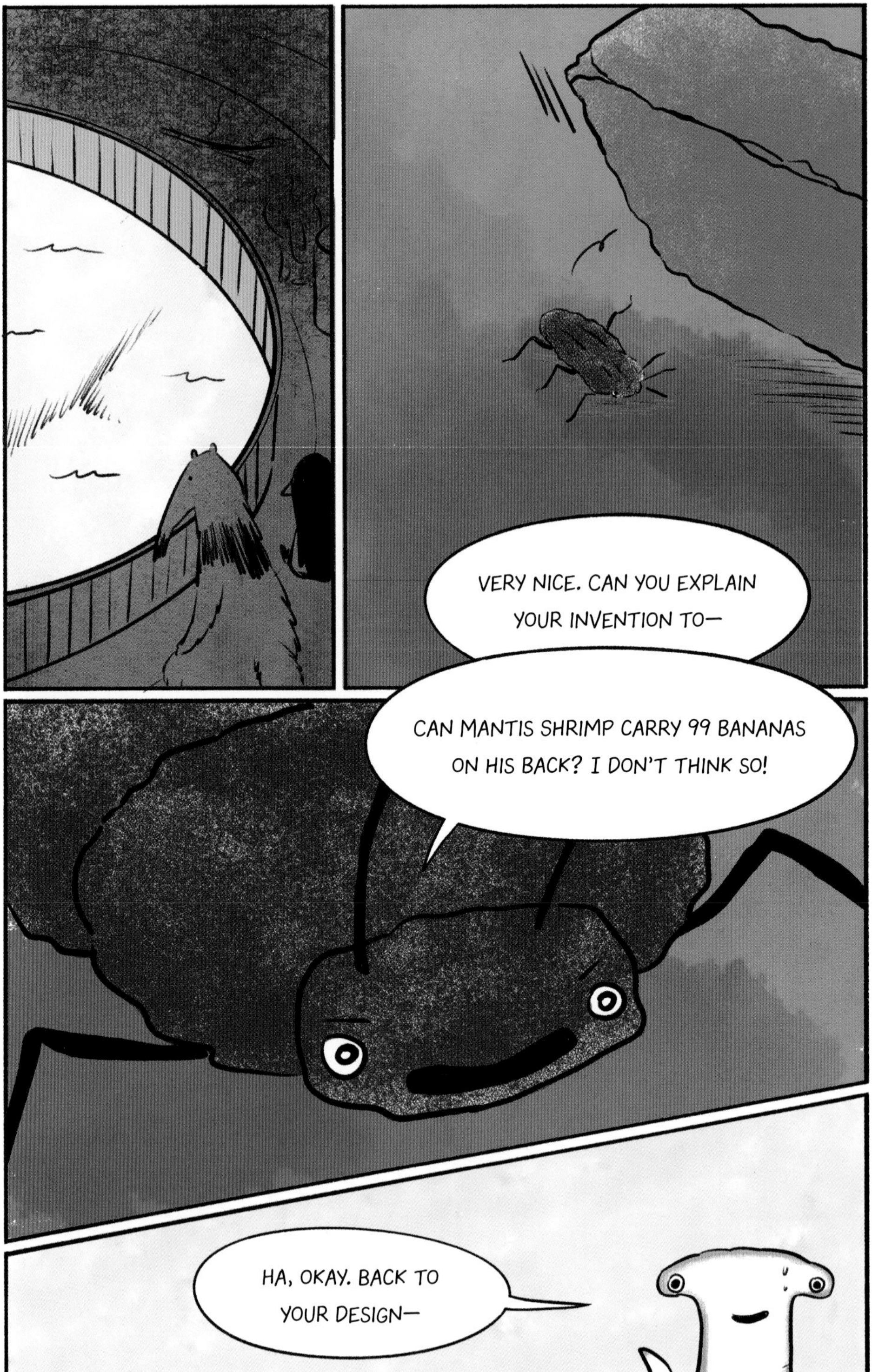
VERY NICE. CAN YOU EXPLAIN YOUR INVENTION TO—
CAN MANTIS SHRIMP CARRY 99 BANANAS ON HIS BACK? I DON'T THINK SO!
HA, OKAY. BACK TO YOUR DESIGN—

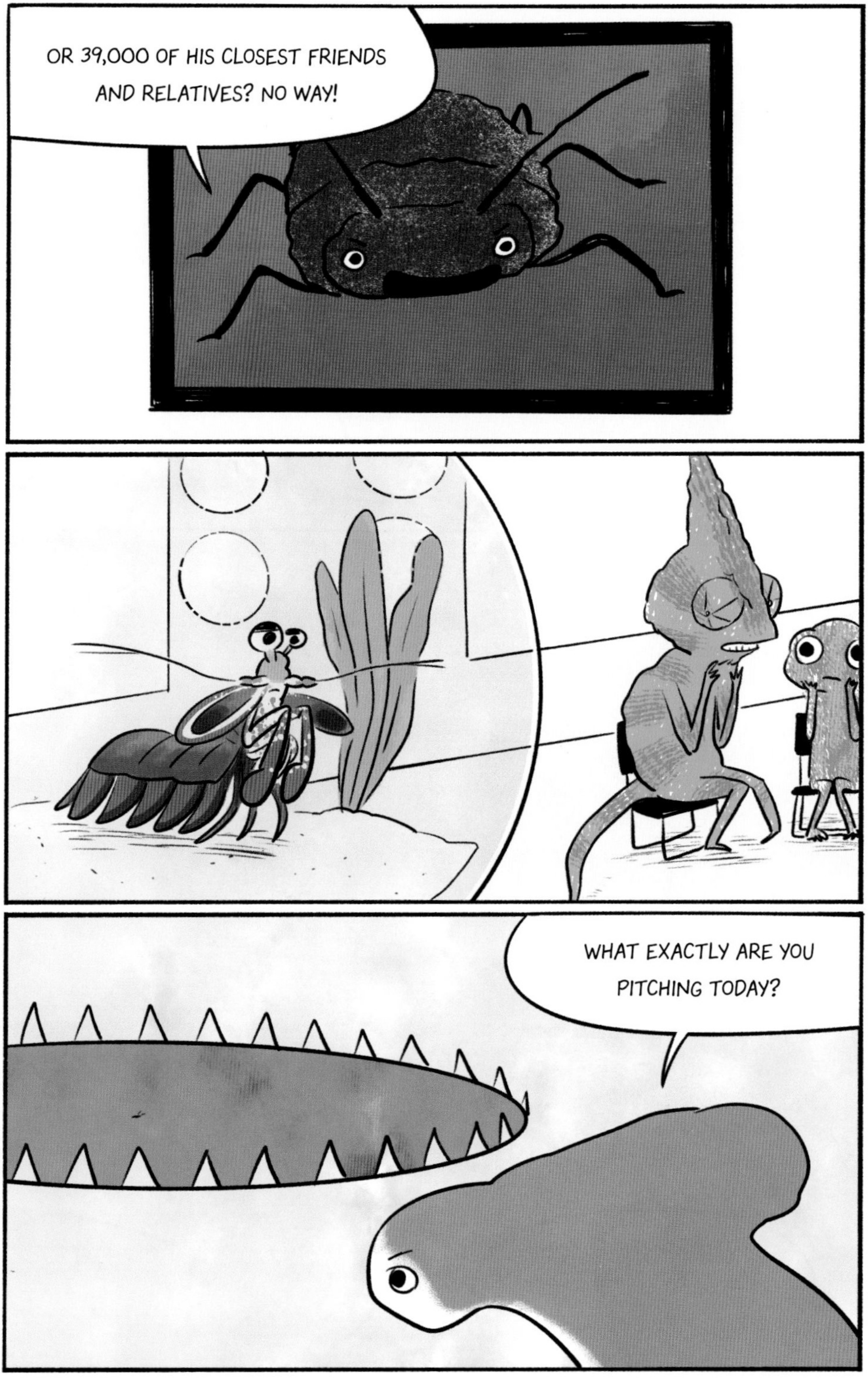
OR 39,000 OF HIS CLOSEST FRIENDS AND RELATIVES? NO WAY!
WHAT EXACTLY ARE YOU PITCHING TODAY?

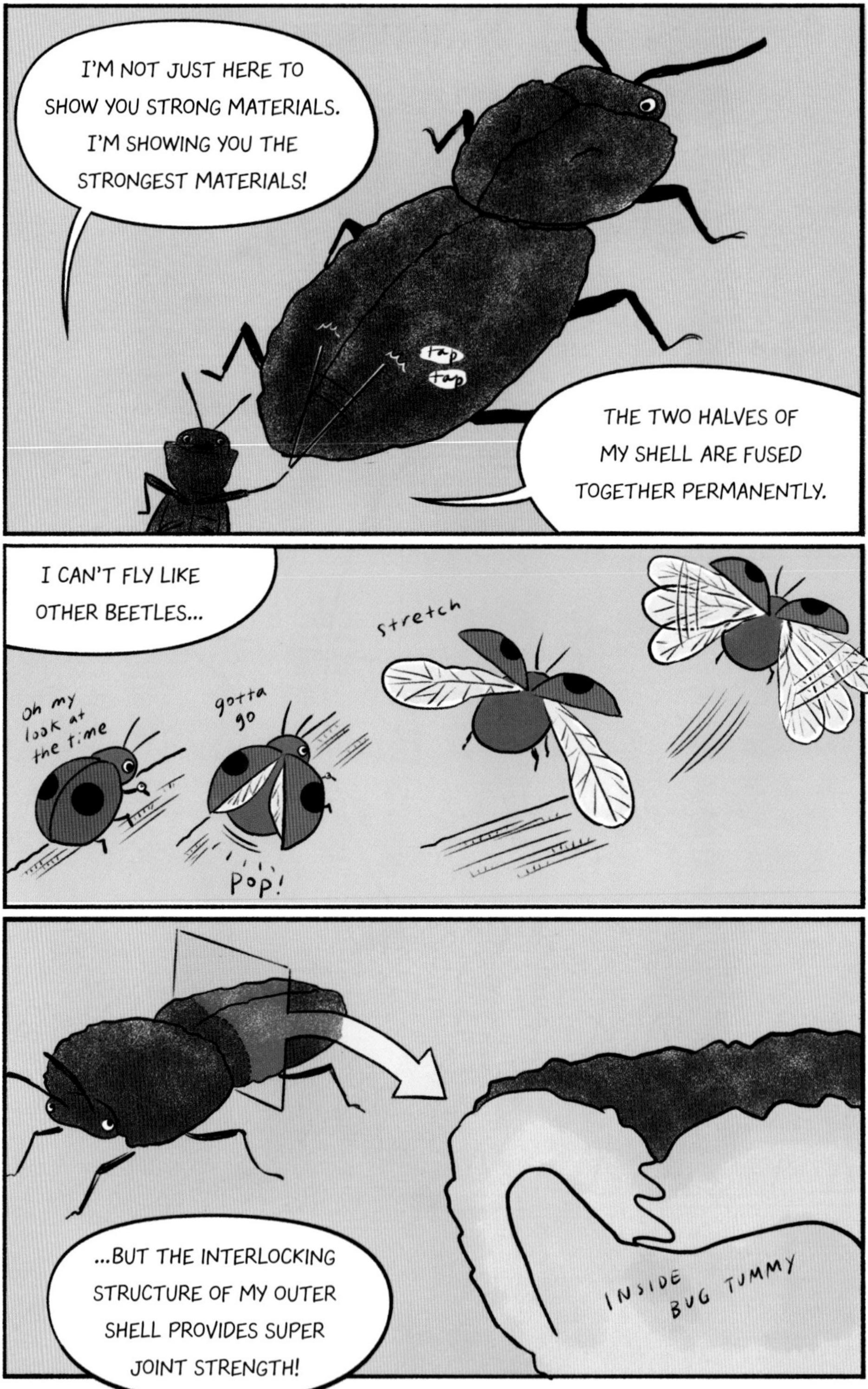
I'M NOT JUST HERE TO SHOW YOU STRONG MATERIALS. I'M SHOWING YOU THE STRONGEST MATERIALS!
tap
tap
THE TWO HALVES OF MY SHELL ARE FUSED TOGETHER PERMANENTLY.
I CAN'T FLY LIKE OTHER BEETLES...
oh my look at the time
gotta go
Pop!
stretch
...BUT THE INTERLOCKING STRUCTURE OF MY OUTER SHELL PROVIDES SUPER JOINT STRENGTH!
INSIDE BUG TUMMY

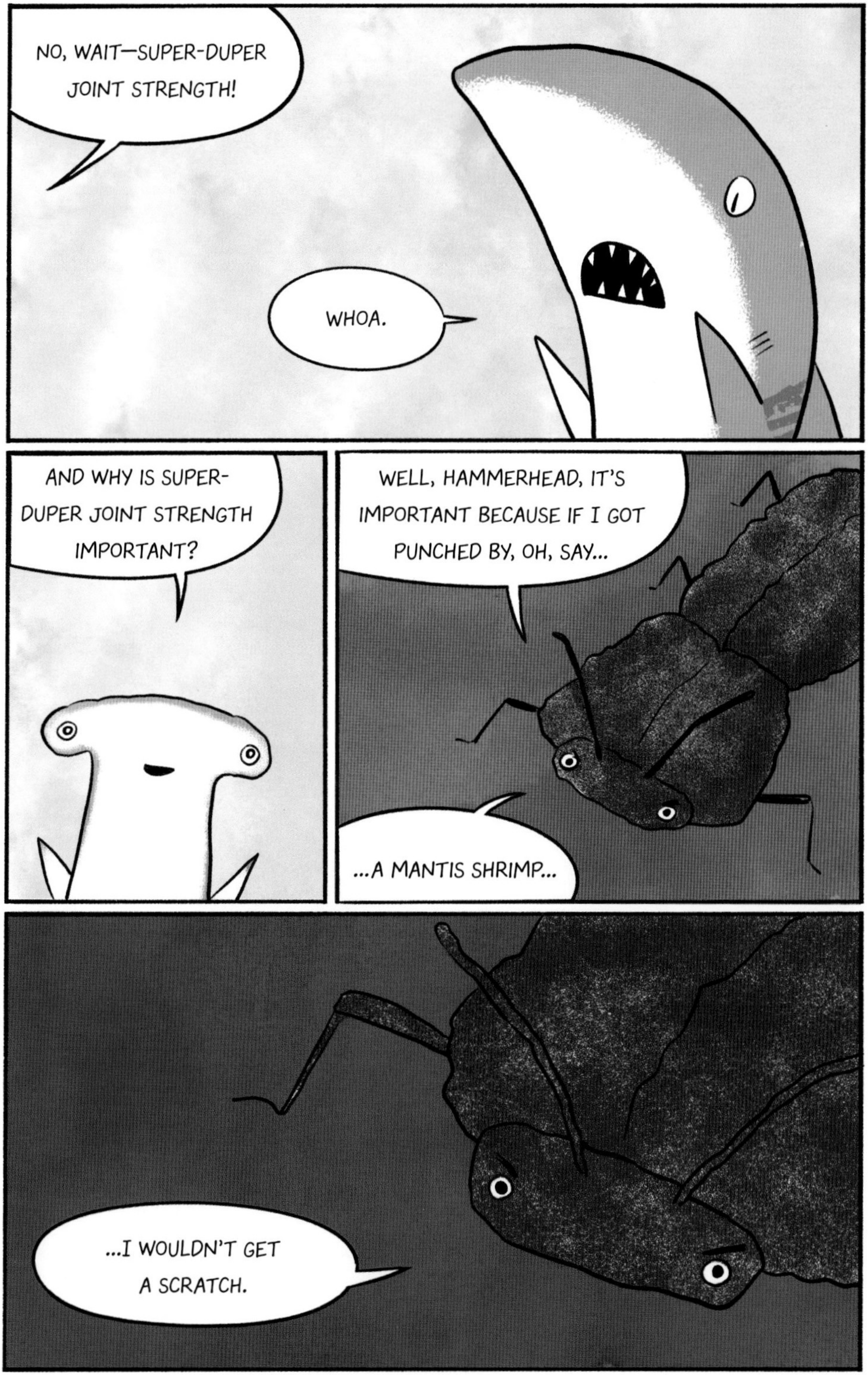
NO, WAIT—SUPER-DUPER JOINT STRENGTH!
WHOA.
AND WHY IS SUPER-DUPER JOINT STRENGTH IMPORTANT?
WELL, HAMMERHEAD, IT'S IMPORTANT BECAUSE IF I GOT PUNCHED BY, OH, SAY...
...A MANTIS SHRIMP...
...I WOULDN'T GET A SCRATCH.

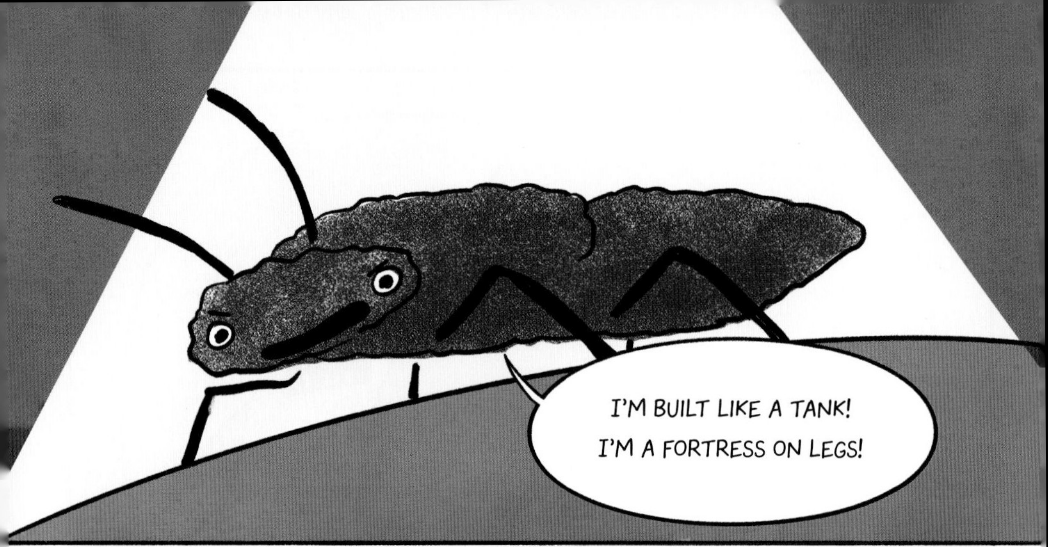
I'M BUILT LIKE A TANK!
I'M A FORTRESS ON LEGS!

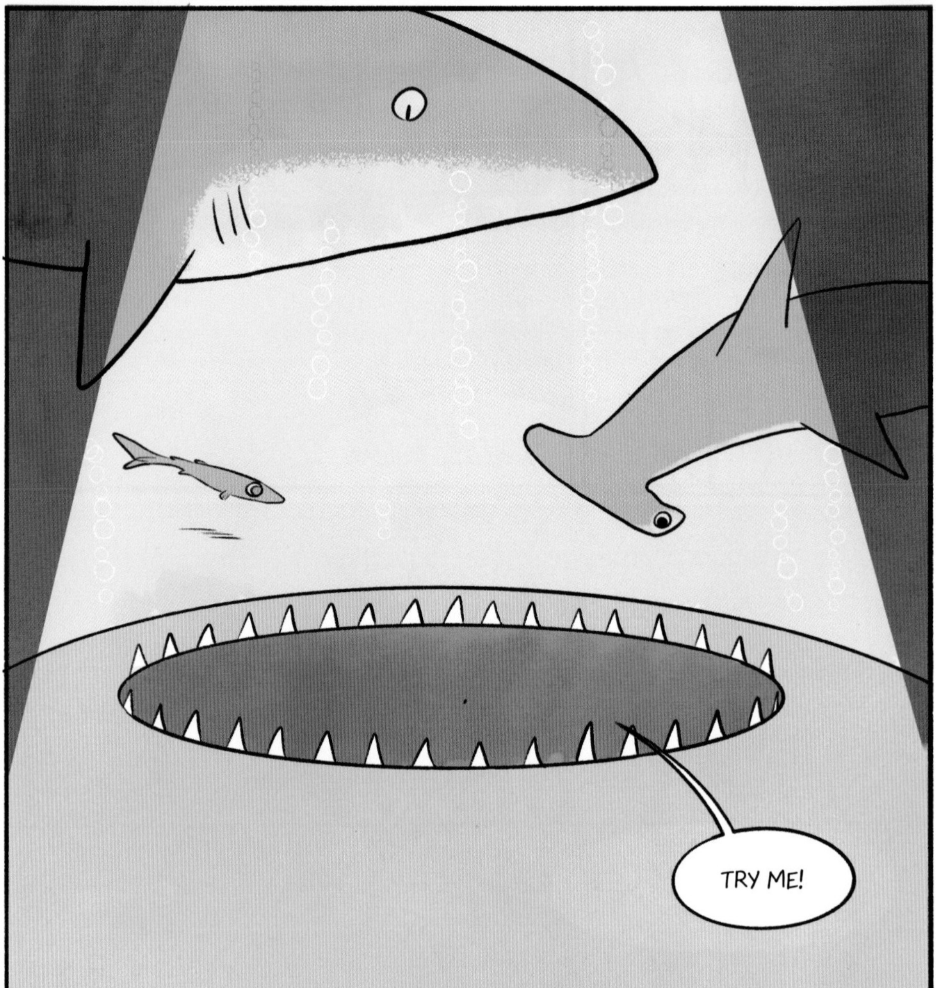
TRY ME!

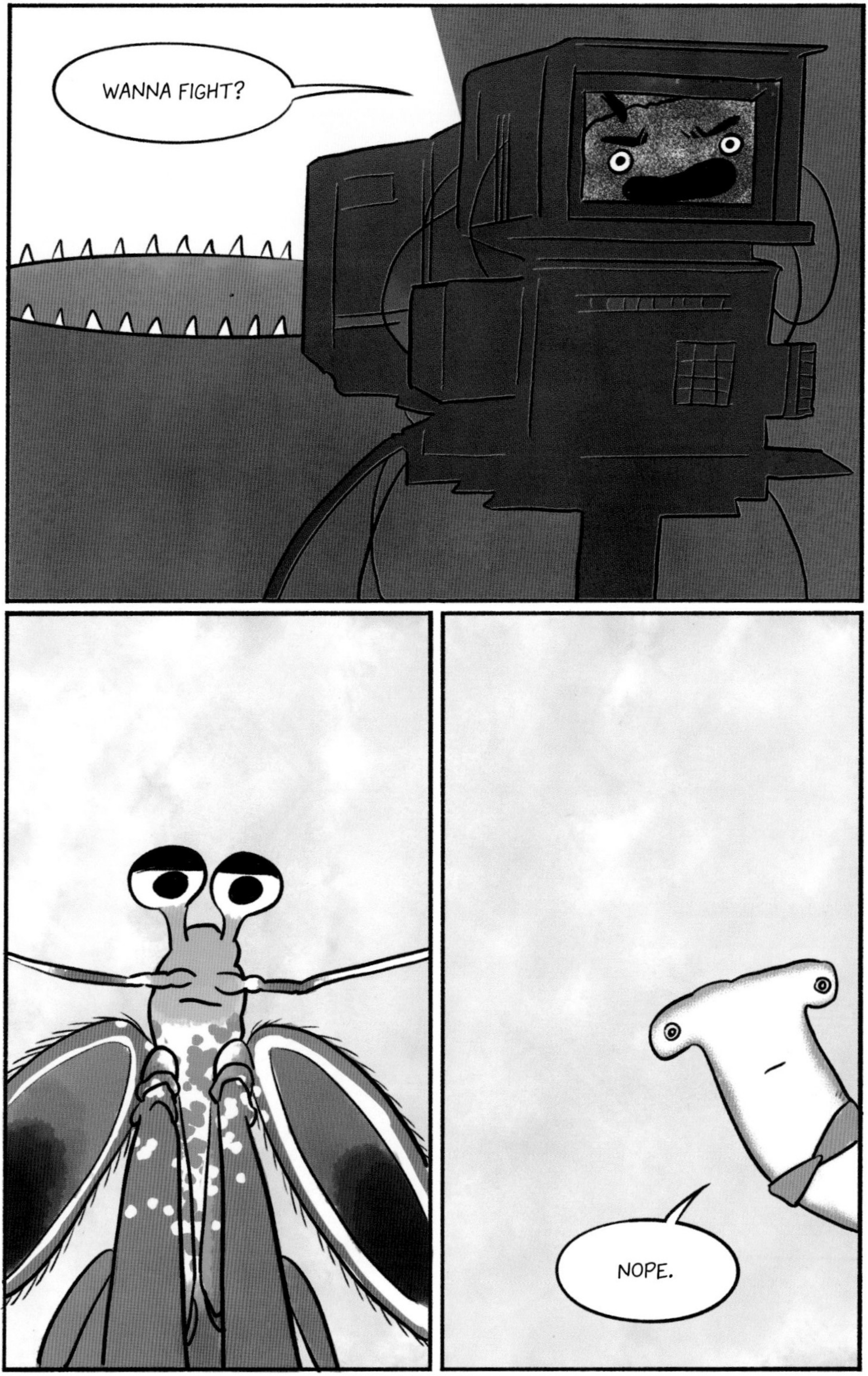
WANNA FIGHT?
NOPE.

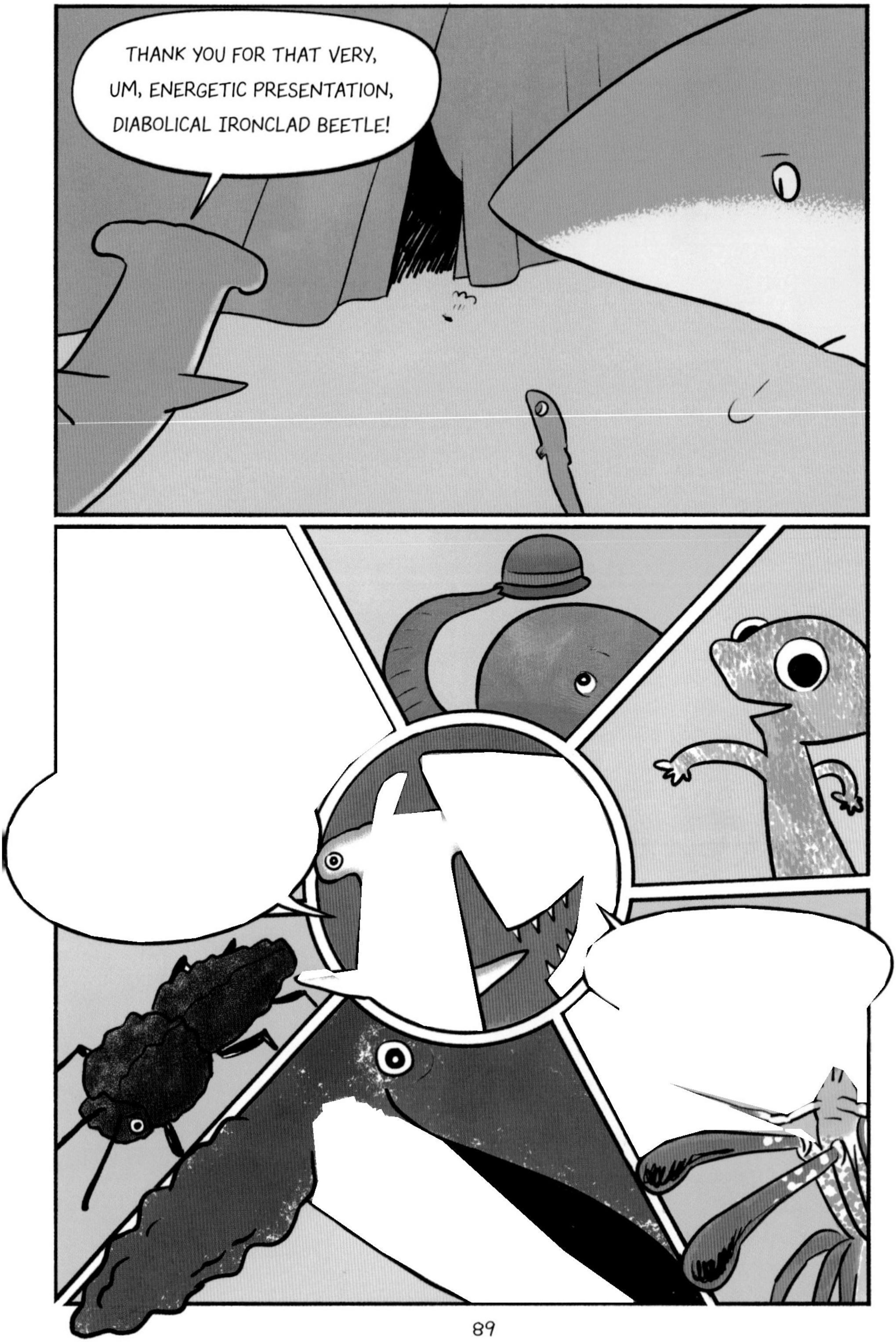
THANK YOU FOR THAT VERY, UM, ENERGETIC PRESENTATION, DIABOLICAL IRONCLAD BEETLE!

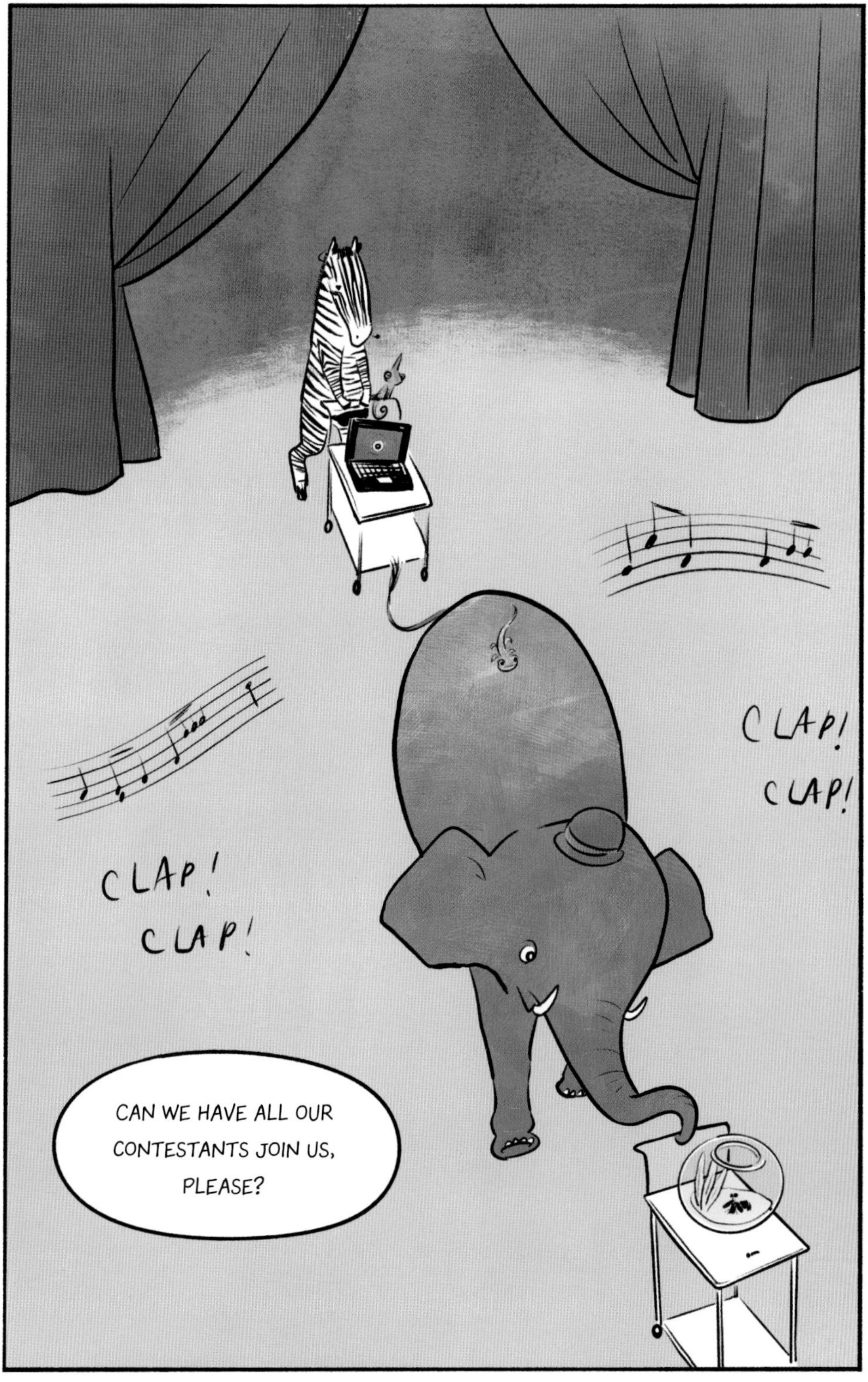
CLAP!
CLAP!
CLAP!
CLAP!
CAN WE HAVE ALL OUR CONTESTANTS JOIN US, PLEASE?

CHAPTER
EIGHT

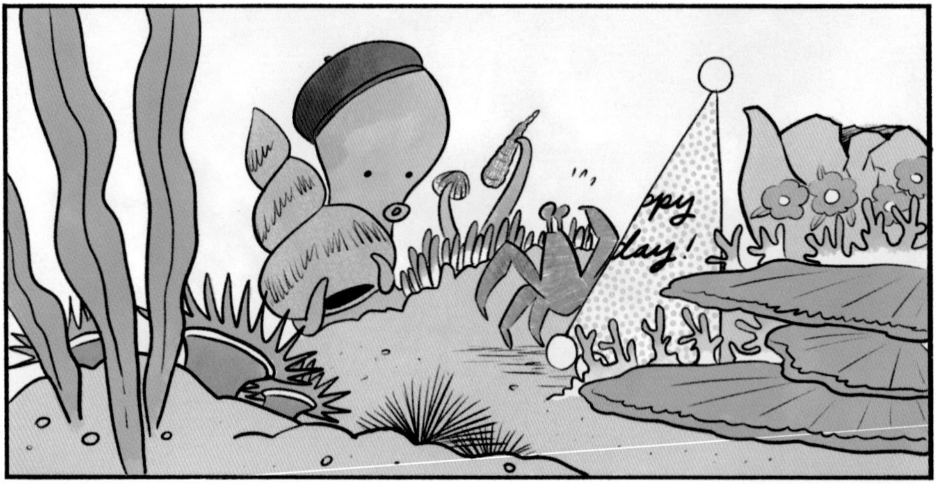
ppy
day!

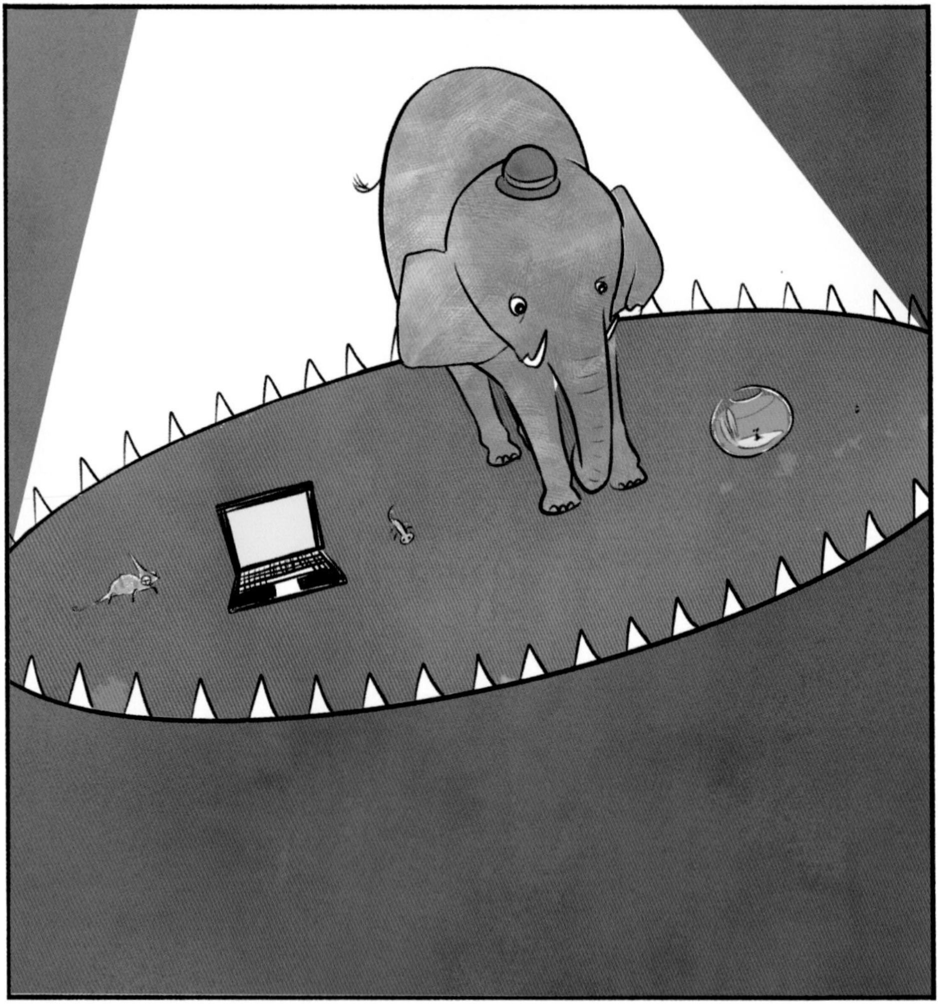

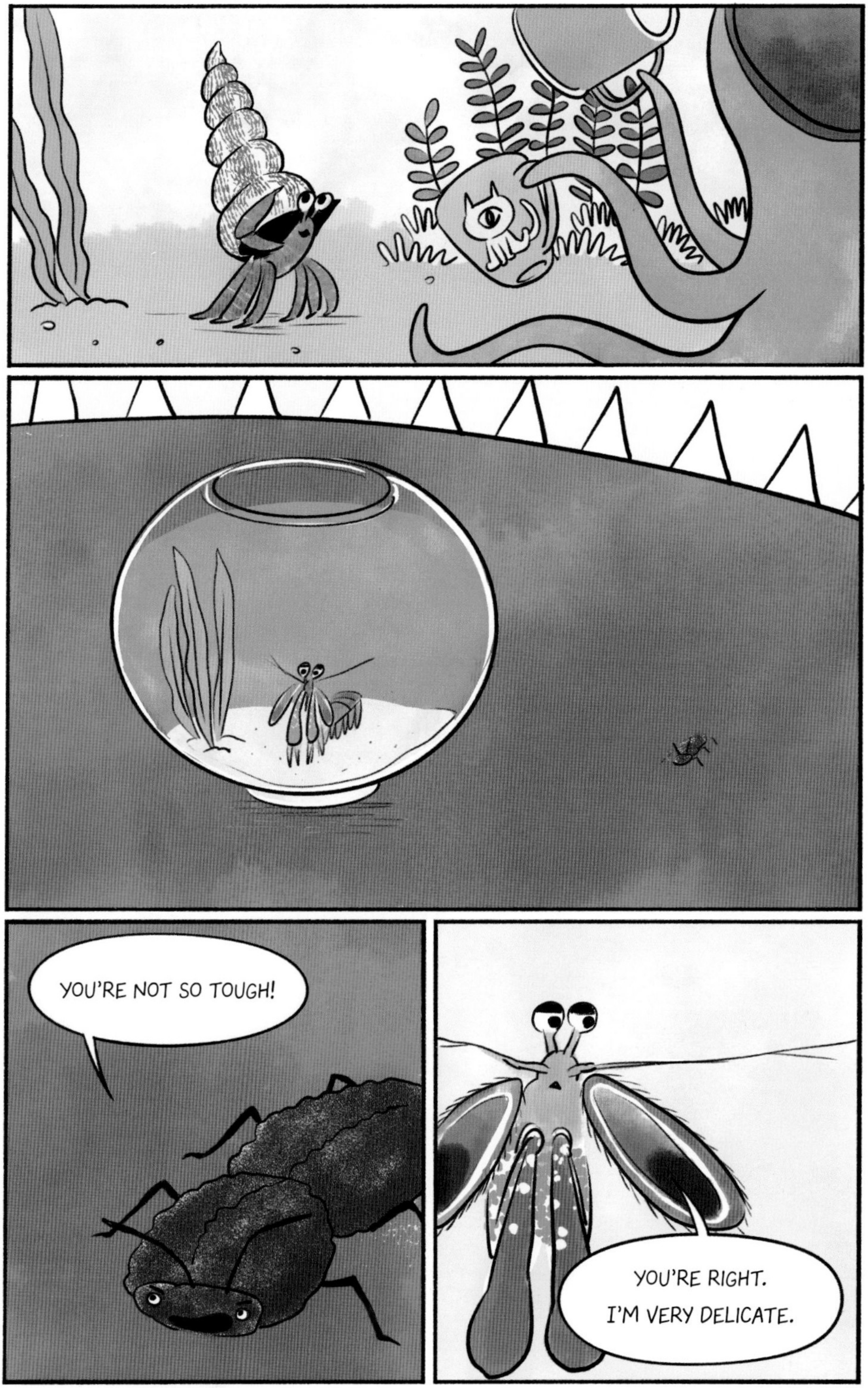
YOU'RE NOT SO TOUGH!
YOU'RE RIGHT. I'M VERY DELICATE.

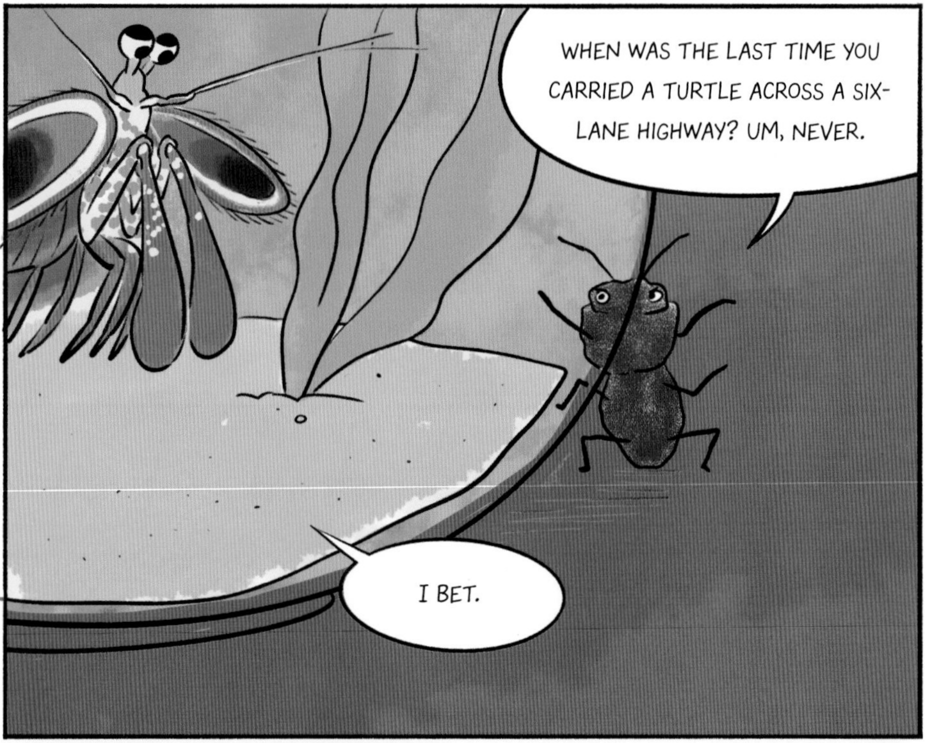
WHEN WAS THE LAST TIME YOU CARRIED A TURTLE ACROSS A SIX-LANE HIGHWAY? UM, NEVER.
I BET.
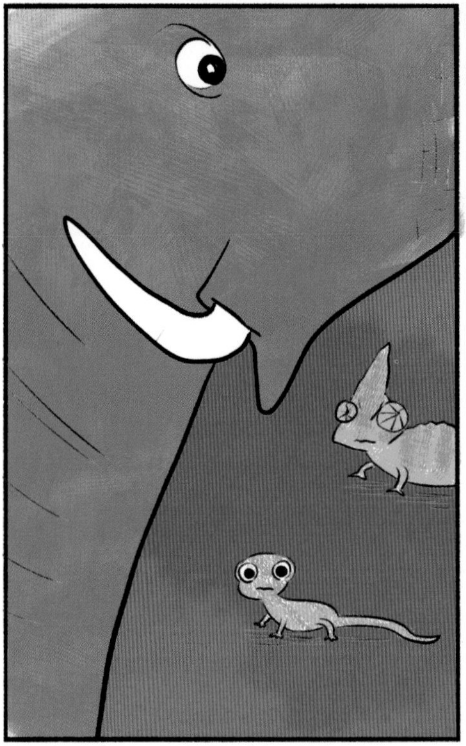
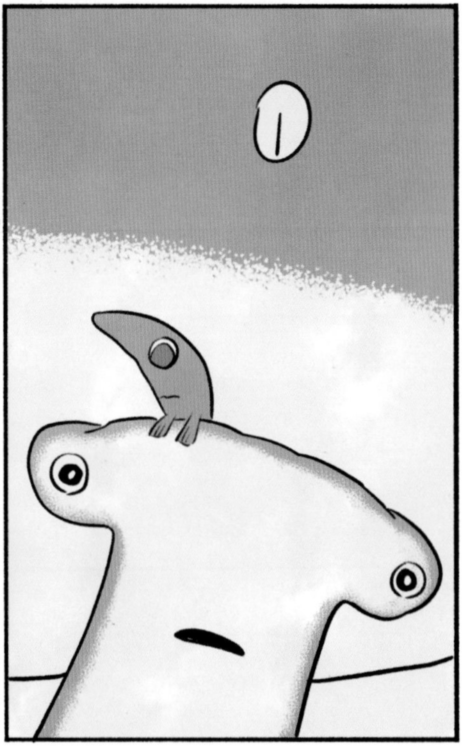

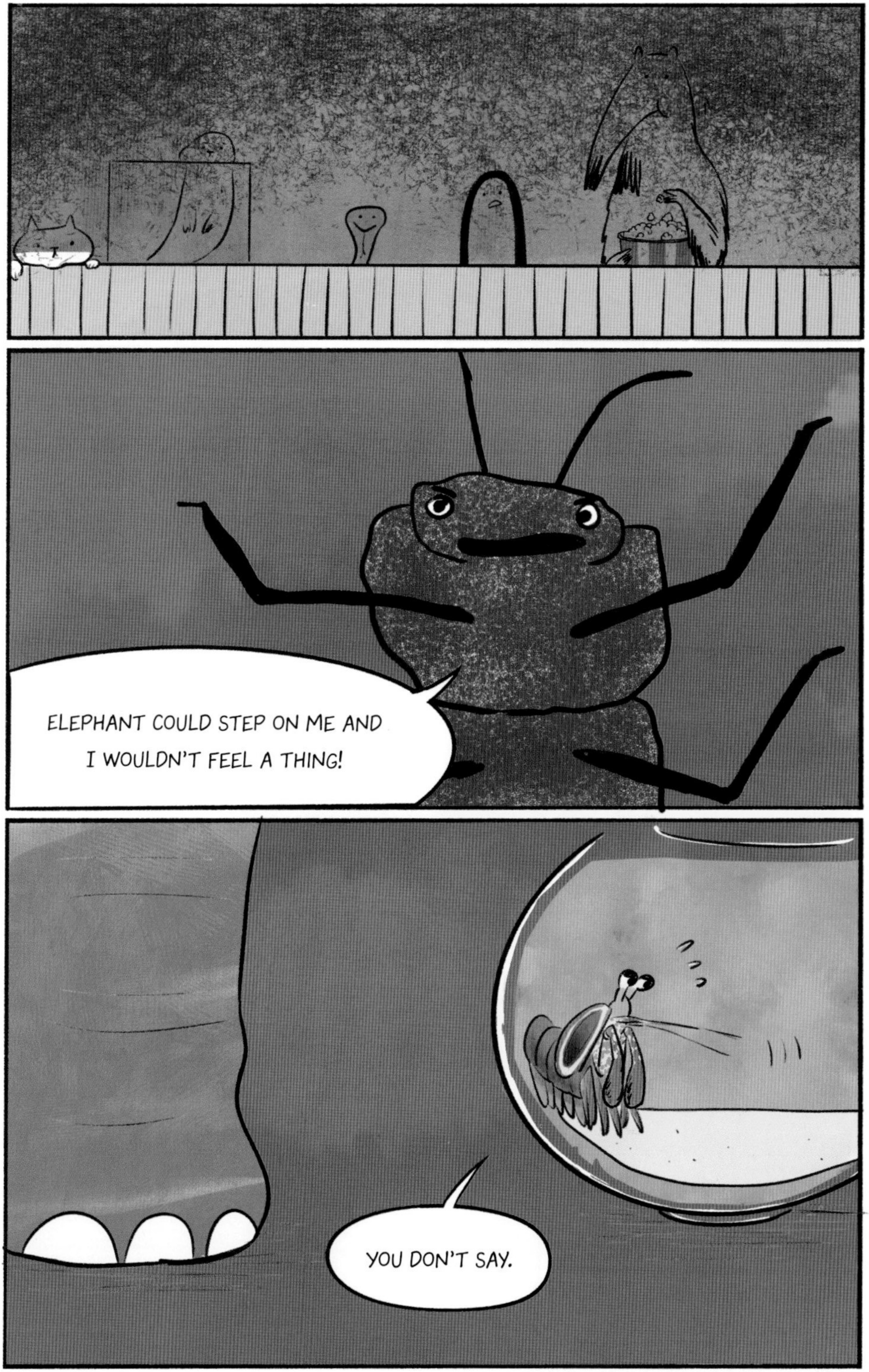
ELEPHANT COULD STEP ON ME AND I WOULDN'T FEEL A THING!
YOU DON'T SAY.

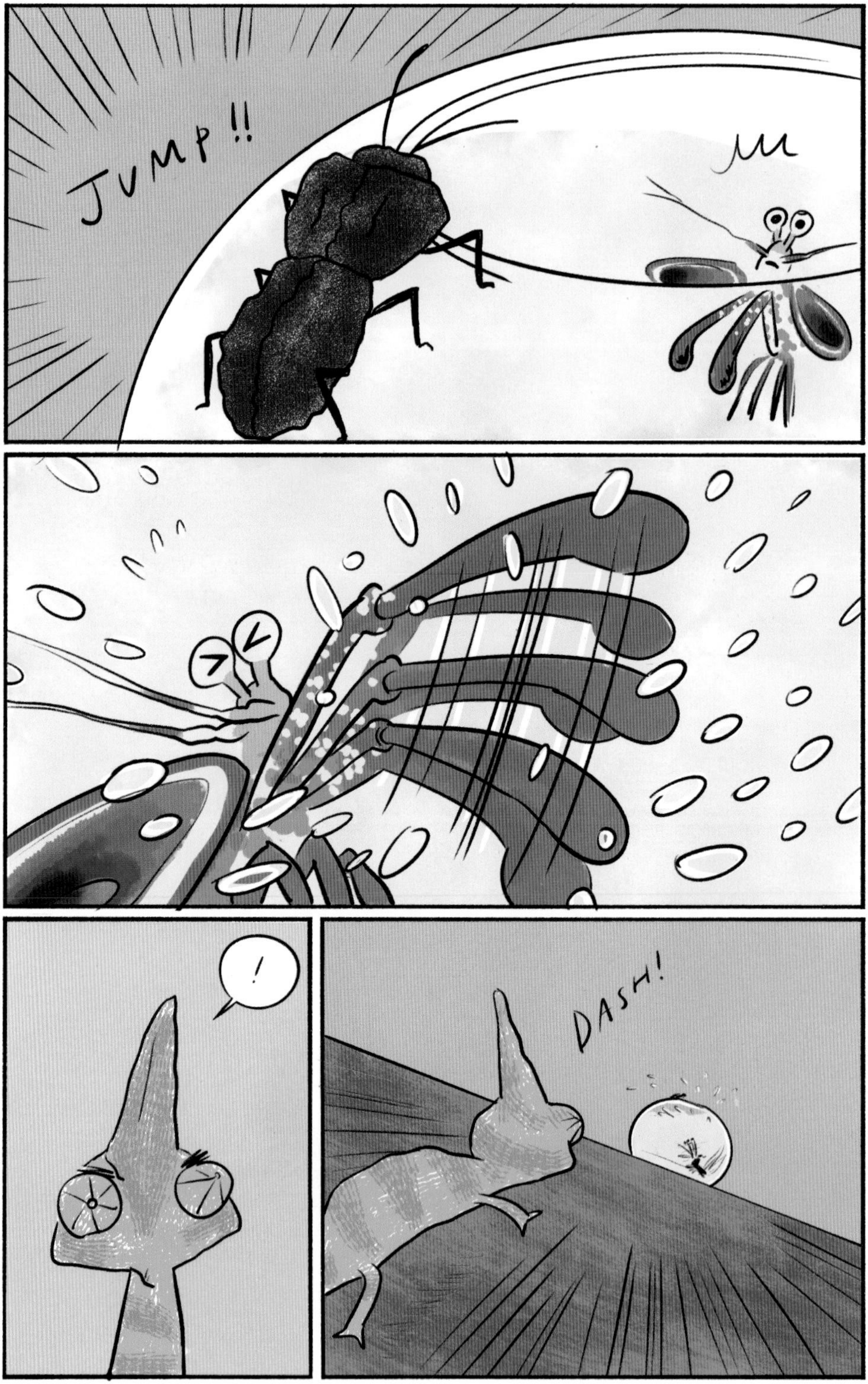
JUMP!!
!
DASH!

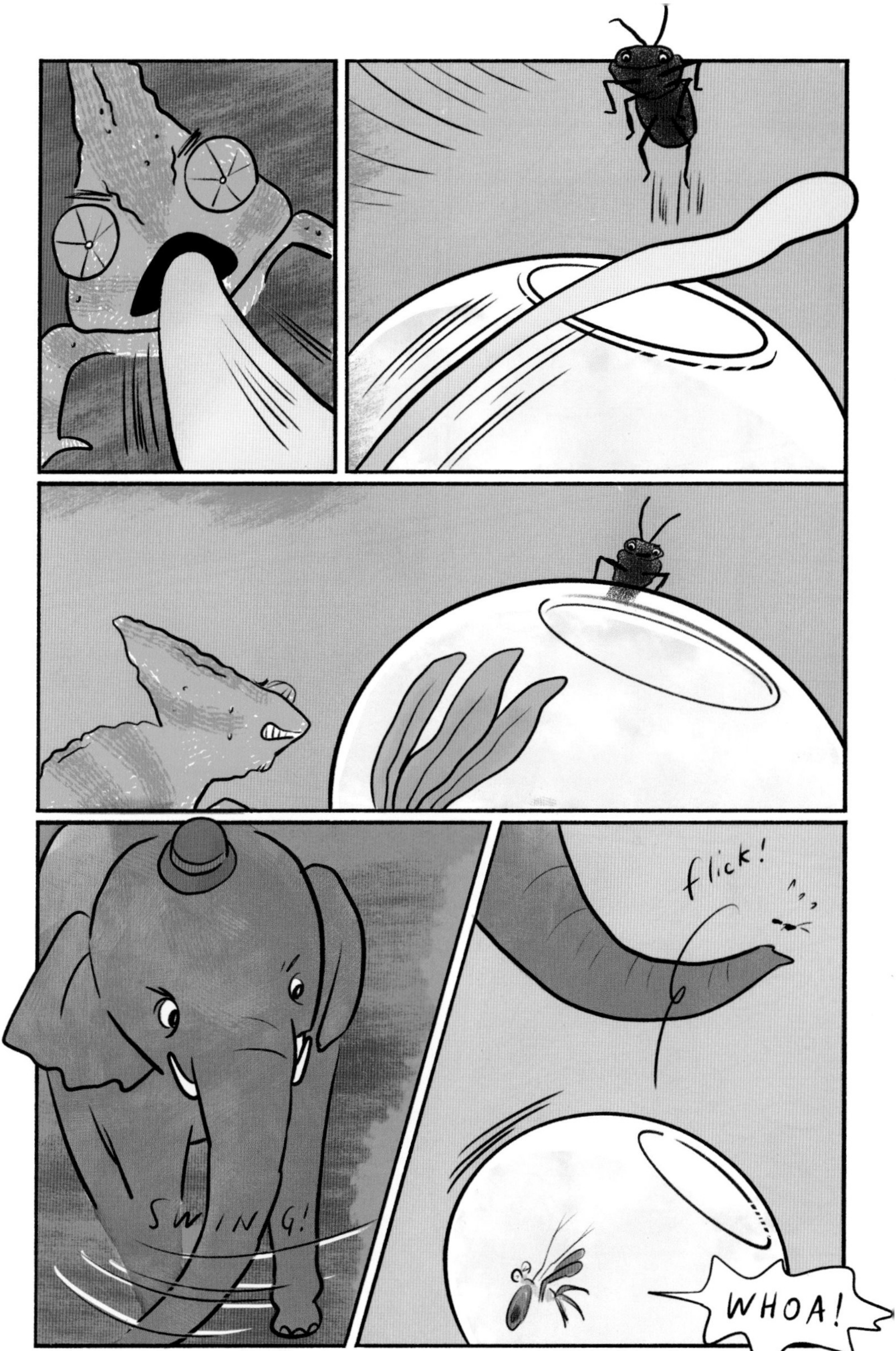
SWING!
flick!
WHOA!

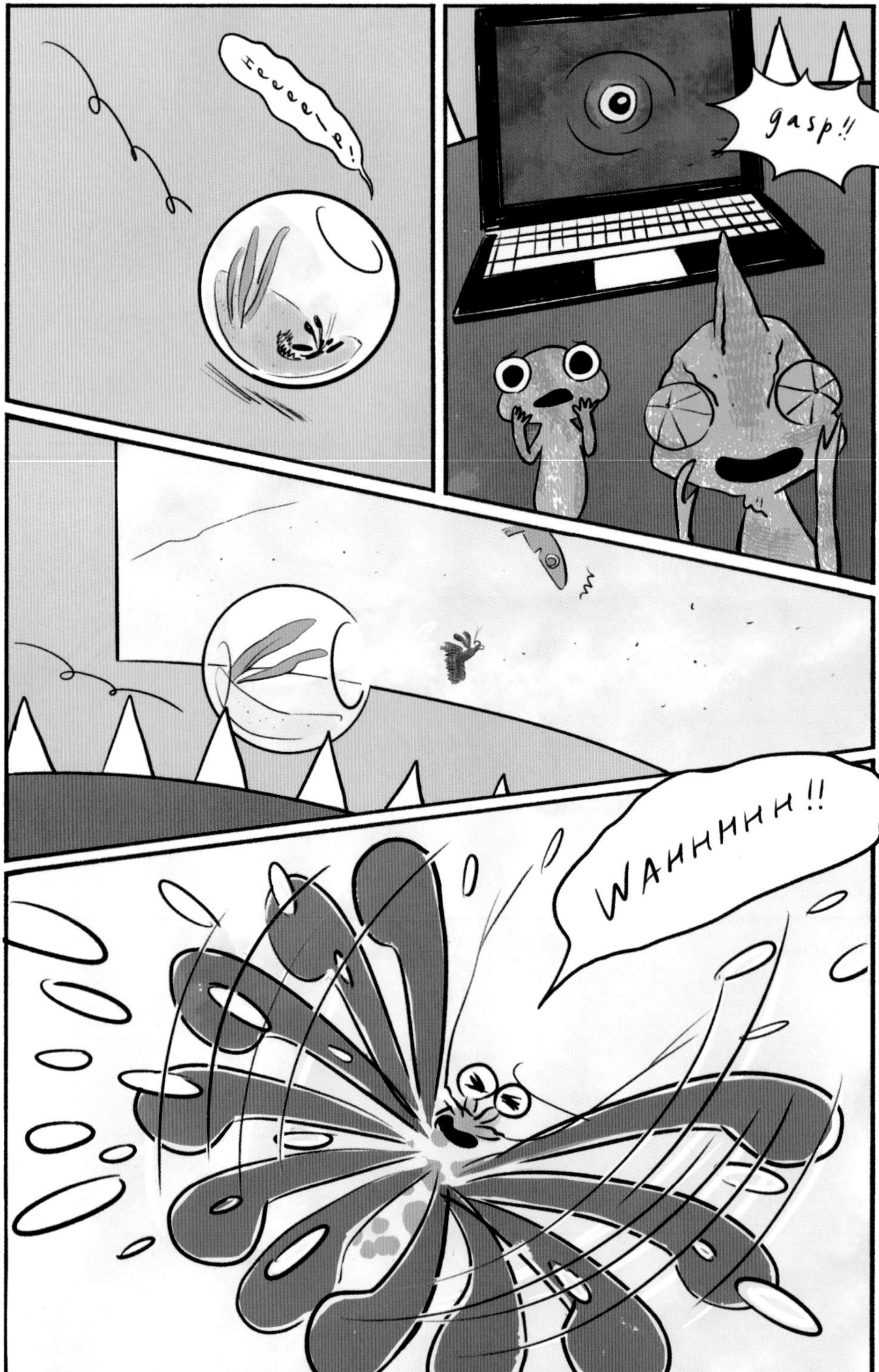
Eeeeeee!
gasp!!
WAHHHHH!!

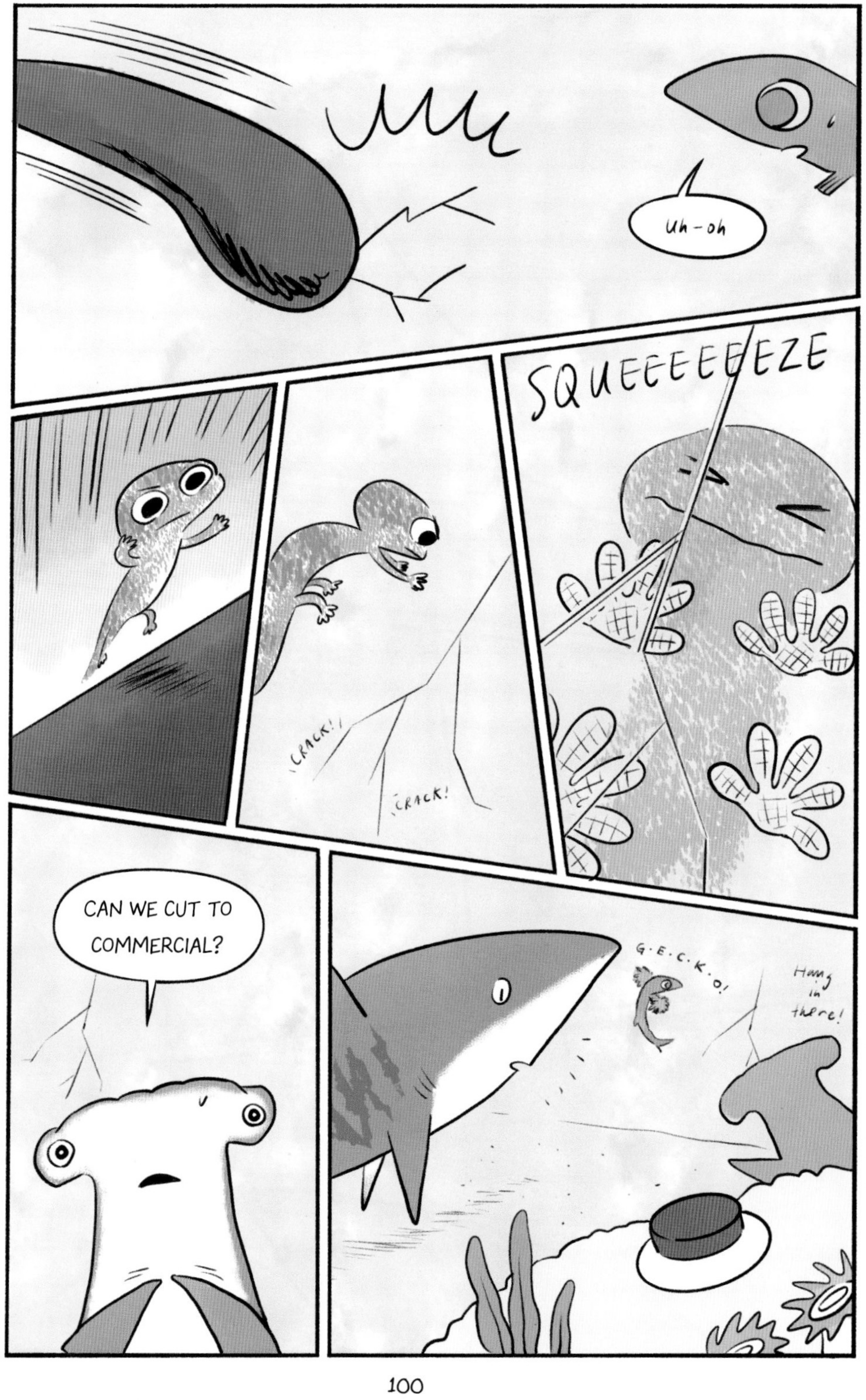
Uh-oh
SQUEEEEEEZE
CRACK!
CRACK!
CAN WE CUT TO COMMERCIAL?
G-E-C-K-O!
Hang in there!

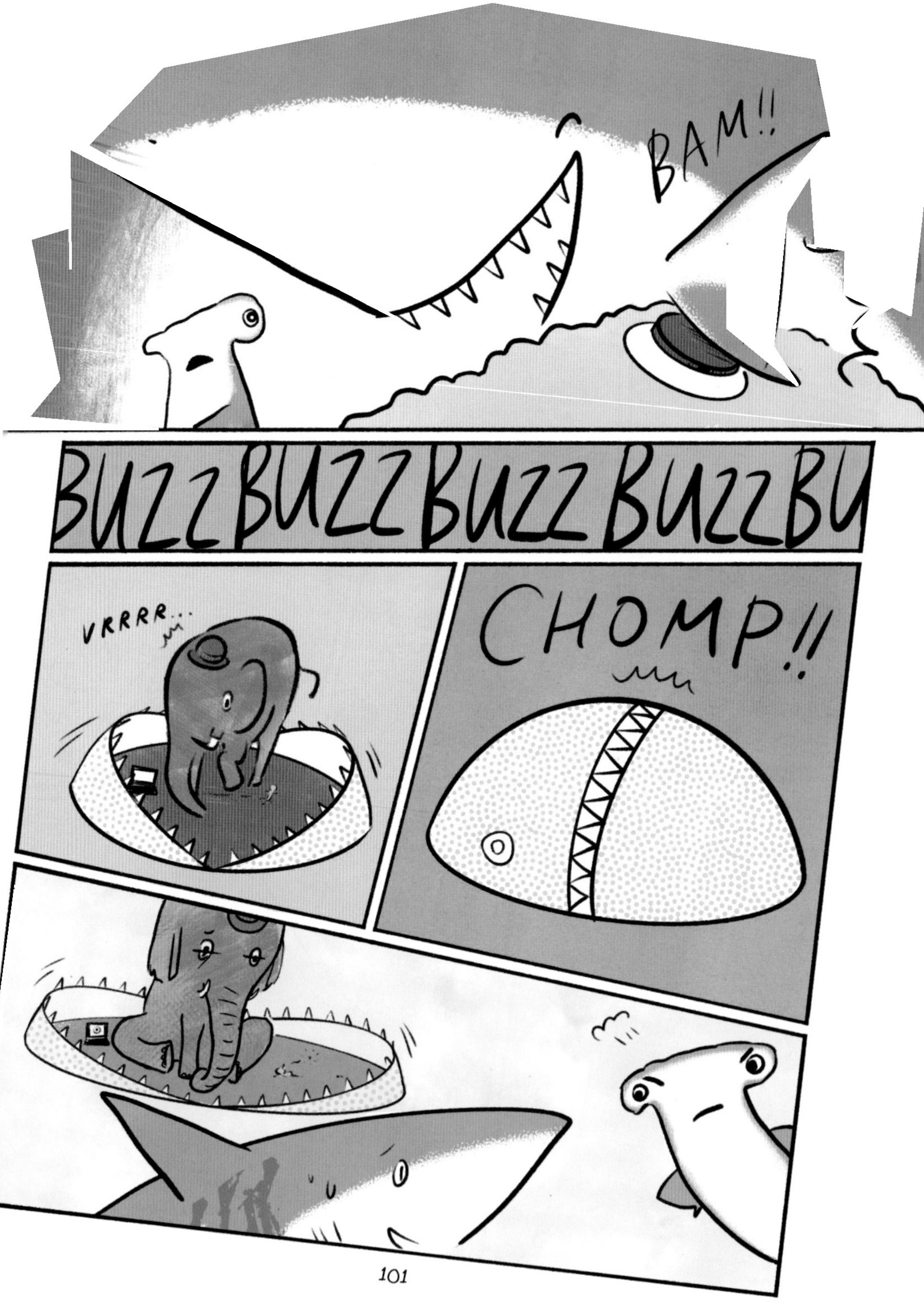
BAM!!
BUZZBUZZBUZZBUZZBU
VRRRR...
CHOMP!!

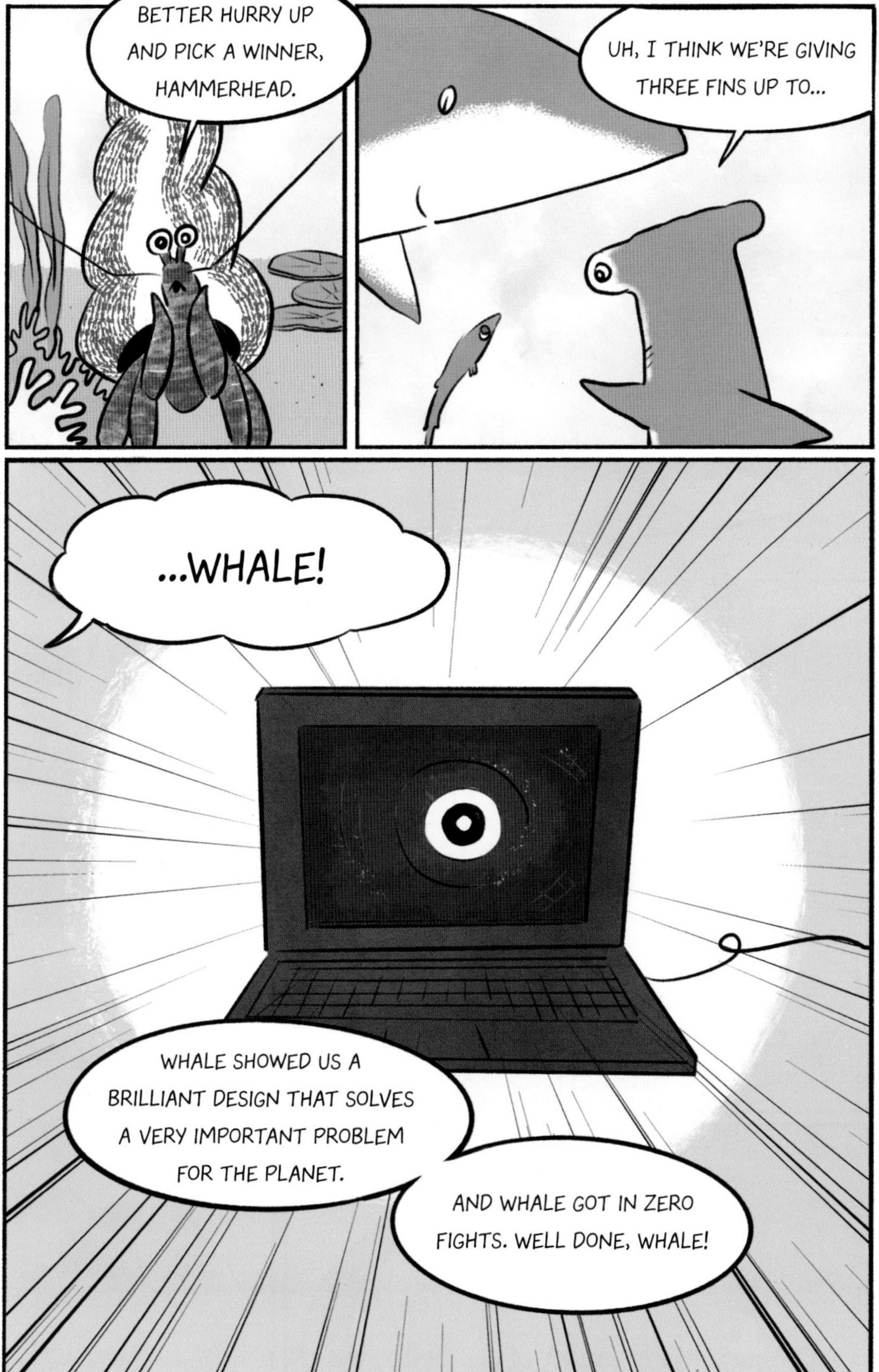
BETTER HURRY UP AND PICK A WINNER, HAMMERHEAD.
UH, I THINK WE'RE GIVING THREE FINS UP TO...
...WHALE!
WHALE SHOWED US A BRILLIANT DESIGN THAT SOLVES A VERY IMPORTANT PROBLEM FOR THE PLANET.
AND WHALE GOT IN ZERO FIGHTS. WELL DONE, WHALE!

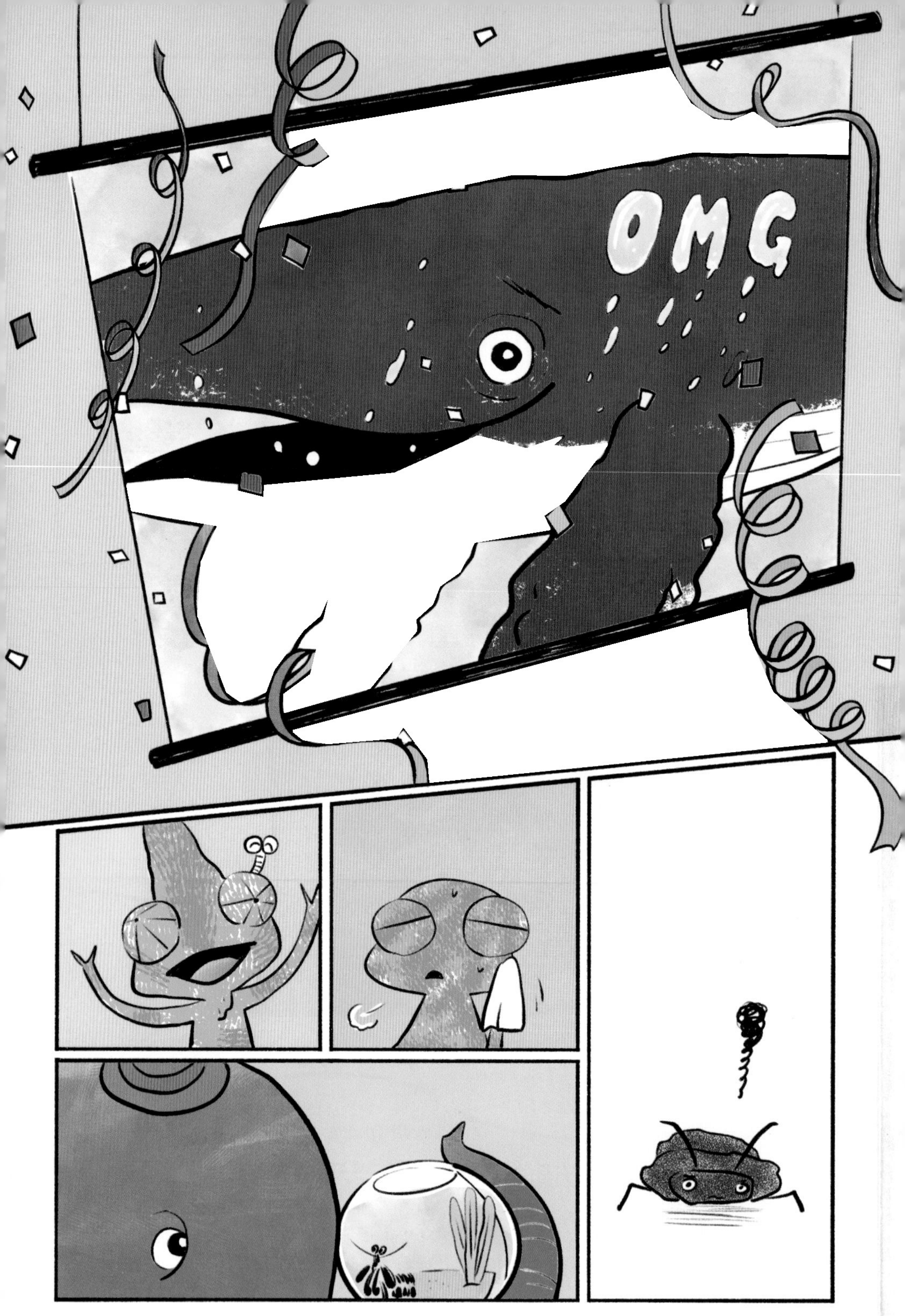
OMG

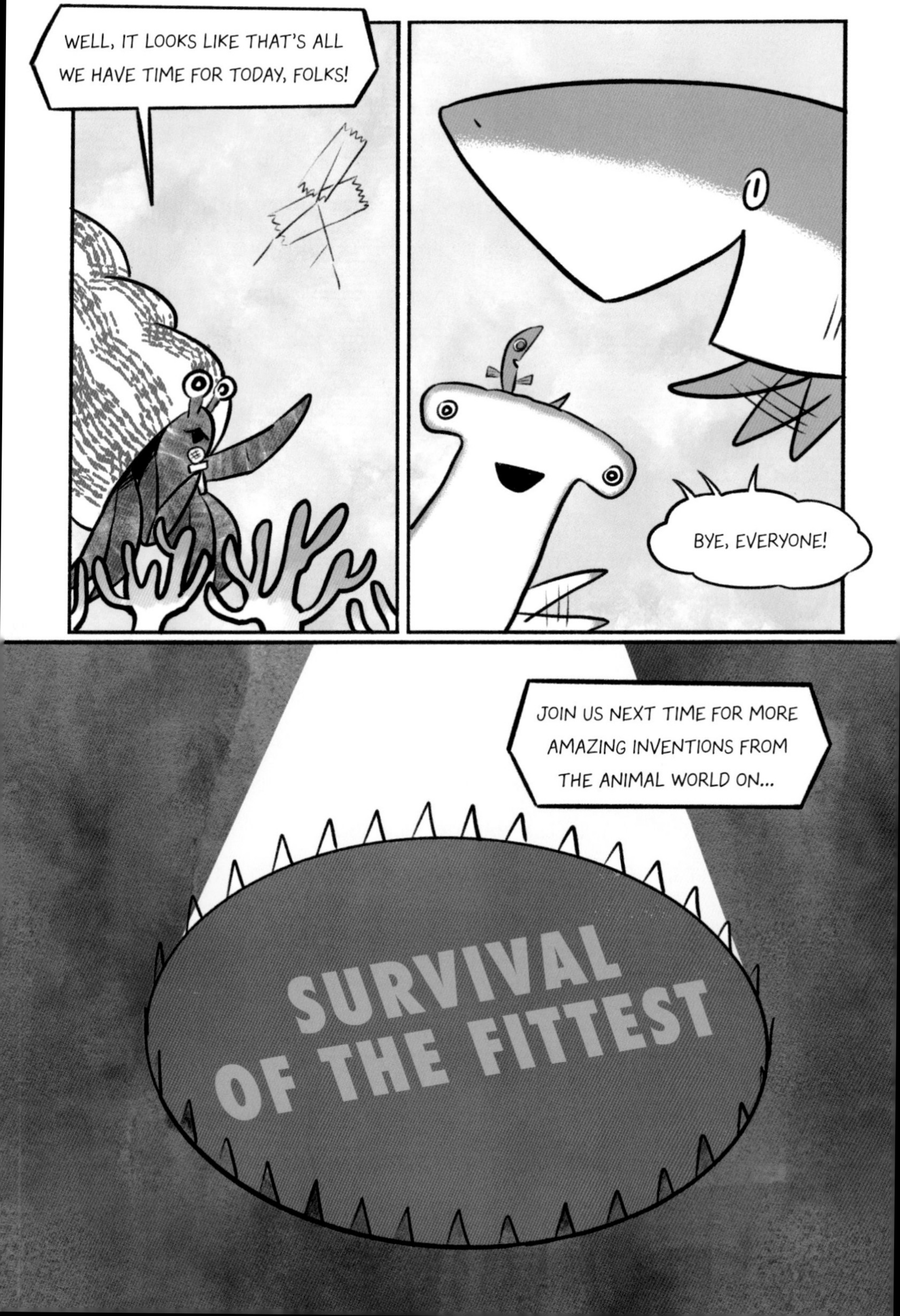
WELL, IT LOOKS LIKE THAT'S ALL WE HAVE TIME FOR TODAY, FOLKS!
BYE, EVERYONE!
JOIN US NEXT TIME FOR MORE AMAZING INVENTIONS FROM THE ANIMAL WORLD ON...
SURVIVAL OF THE FITTEST

THE DESIGNS

WE HAVE A LOT TO LEARN FROM HOW NATURE SOLVES PROBLEMS. ALL THE INVENTIONS ON *SURVIVAL OF THE FITTEST* ARE REAL IDEAS BASED ON ANIMALS' AMAZING ABILITIES! SOME OF THEM HAVE BEEN MADE INTO PRODUCTS, AND SOME ARE JUST SKETCHES OR MODELS. JUST AS HERMIT CRAB SAID, NATURE WAS THE FIRST—AND BEST—INVENTOR.

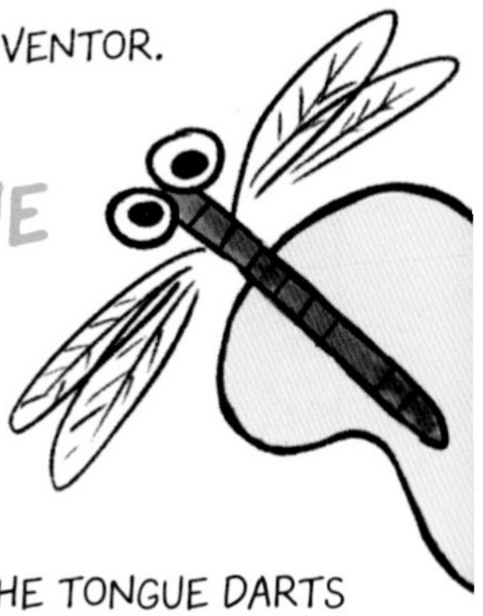

CHAMELEON'S SQUISHY TONGUE

IMAGINE HAVING TO CATCH ALL YOUR FOOD WITH YOUR TONGUE! YOU'D WANT IT TO BE FAST AND FLEXIBLE AND TO GRIP LIKE A PRO WRESTLER. BUT HOW EXACTLY DOES A CHAMELEON'S TONGUE CAPTURE INSECTS? AS THE TIP OF THE TONGUE DARTS TOWARD A TASTY BUG, THE MIDDLE MOVES BACK SLIGHTLY WHILE THE EDGES KEEP MOVING FORWARD, LETTING THE TONGUE MOLD AROUND WHATEVER IT'S GOING AFTER. THIS CONCEPT WORKS SO WELL, A NORWEGIAN DESIGN TEAM USED IT TO CREATE THE FLEXSHAPEGRIPPER. BECAUSE IT DOESN'T HAVE ANY SHARP EDGES, IT CAN SAFELY PICK UP EVEN THE MOST DELICATE OBJECTS.

READ MORE: PRESS.FESTO.COM/EN/TECHNOLOGIES-AND-PRODUCTS-1/THE-AUTOMATED-CHAMELEON-TONGUE

WHALE'S BUMPY FLIPPER

JUST LIKE IN THE CONTEST, WHALE'S FLIPPER IS A REAL WINNER. A CANADIAN COMPANY CALLED WHALEPOWER PATENTED A TECHNOLOGY BASED ON THE FLIPPER'S BUMPS, OR TUBERCLES. IT'S BEEN USED TO MAKE COOLING FANS

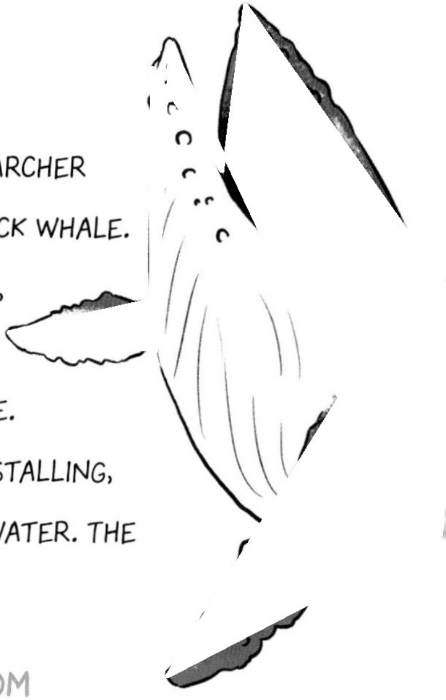

INSIDE DIESEL ENGINES AND DIGITAL DEVICES. A RESEARCHER GOT THE IDEA WHEN HE SAW A STATUE OF A HUMPBACK WHALE. HE NOTICED THAT THE LEADING, OR FORWARD-FACING, EDGE OF THE FLIPPER WAS BUMPY. MOST LEADING EDGES ARE SMOOTH, LIKE THE WINGS ON AN AIRPLANE. IT TURNS OUT THE BUMPS CUT DOWN ON DRAG AND STALLING, LETTING WHALES MOVE MORE EASILY THROUGH THE WATER. THE RESEARCHER'S NAME? DR. FRANK FISH—NO JOKE!

READ MORE: WHALEPOWERCORP.WORDPRESS.COM

GECKO'S STICKY FEET

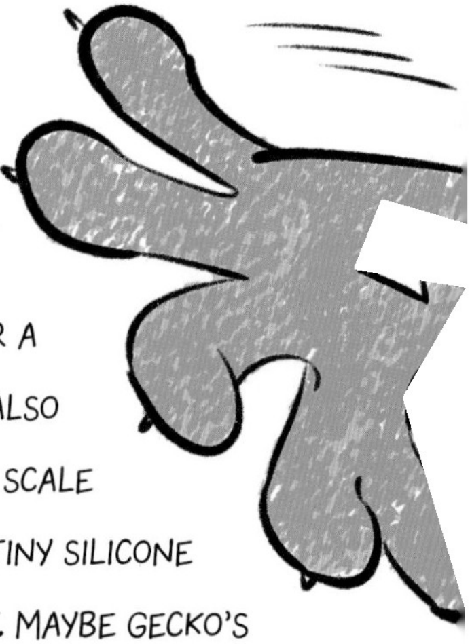

GECKO'S PITCH FOR AN ADHESIVE THAT WORKS IN OUTER SPACE ISN'T THE ONLY TECHNOLOGY INSPIRED BY HIS SUPER GRIPPING POWERS. THE TEAM OF RESEARCHERS AT STANFORD UNIVERSITY THAT CAME UP WITH THE IDEA FOR A "SPACE GARBAGE TRUCK" TO CLEAN UP FLOATING TRASH ALSO DEVELOPED A CLIMBING TECHNOLOGY THAT LETS HUMANS SCALE GLASS BUILDINGS! THE DEVICE USES TILES COVERED WITH TINY SILICONE HAIRS THAT ACT LIKE THE NANOHAIRS ON A GECKO'S FOOT. MAYBE GECKO'S NEXT DESIGN SHOULD BE A SUPERHERO COSTUME: LOOK UP—IT'S GECKO-MAN!

READ MORE: LIVESCIENCE.COM/48845-GECKO-INSPIRED-TECH-CLIMBING-WALLS.HTML

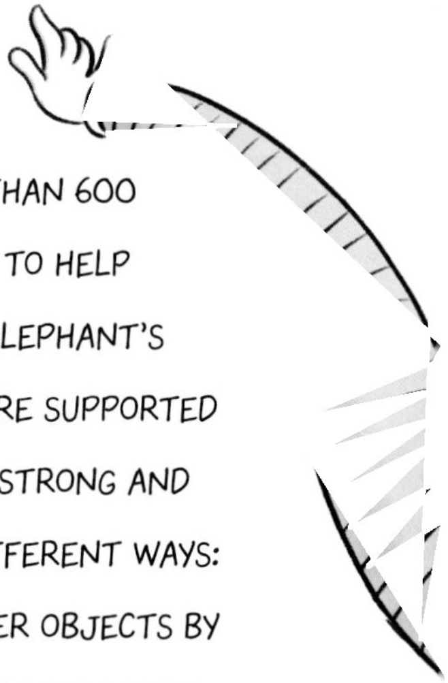

ELEPHANT'S BENDY TRUNK

YOU HAVE OVER 200 BONES IN YOUR BODY AND MORE THAN 600 MUSCLES. YOUR MUSCLES AND BONES WORK TOGETHER TO HELP YOU MOVE BY PULLING AGAINST EACH OTHER, BUT AN ELEPHANT'S TRUNK HAS NO BONES AT ALL. ITS 40,000 MUSCLES ARE SUPPORTED BY WATER! THIS UNIQUE DESIGN MAKES A TRUNK BOTH STRONG AND FLEXIBLE. A TRUNK CAN MOVE AND HOLD THINGS IN DIFFERENT WAYS: USING SUCTION FOR LIGHT OBJECTS OR GRIPPING HEAVIER OBJECTS BY WRAPPING AROUND THEM. A TRUNK CAN EVEN BEND IN A WAY THAT MAKES IT LOOK LIKE IT HAS A JOINT LIKE YOUR ELBOW!

READ MORE: SCIENCEDAILY.COM/RELEASES/2021/08/210823125830.HTM

PEACOCK MANTIS SHRIMP'S FIGHTING CLUB

PEACOCK MANTIS SHRIMP REALLY DID PUNCH HIS WAY OUT OF AN AQUARIUM ONCE! HE USES HIS CLUB TO ATTACK SHELLFISH, CRACKING THEIR SHELLS WITH A BLOW THAT MOVES SO FAST, THE WATER AROUND IT BOILS. BUT THAT'S NOT MANTIS SHRIMP'S ONLY SUPERPOWER: HIS COMPOUND EYES CAN *SEE* CANCER CELLS BEFORE A PATIENT SHOWS ANY SIGNS OF DISEASE. THAT'S BECAUSE HE CAN SEE THE WAY CANCER CELLS REFLECT LIGHT, SOMETHING OUR HUMAN EYES CAN'T DO. ONE MORE FUN FACT: PEACOCK MANTIS SHRIMP IS MORE CLOSELY RELATED TO CRABS AND LOBSTERS—HE'S NOT SUCH A SHRIMP AFTER ALL!

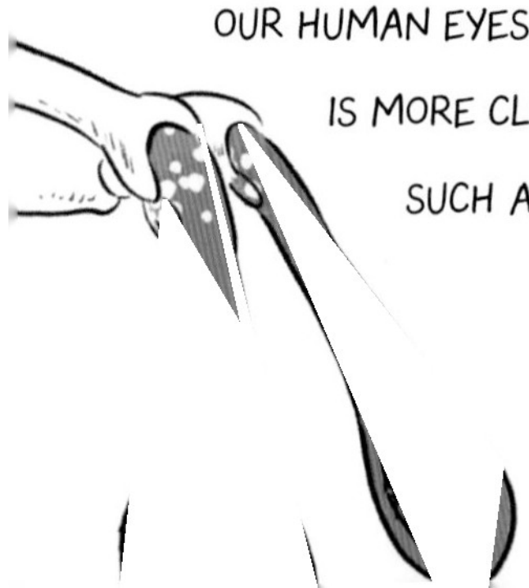

READ MORE: SCIENCEALERT.COM/MANTIS-SHRIMP-CAN-SEE-CANCER-BEFORE-SYMPTOMS-APPEAR

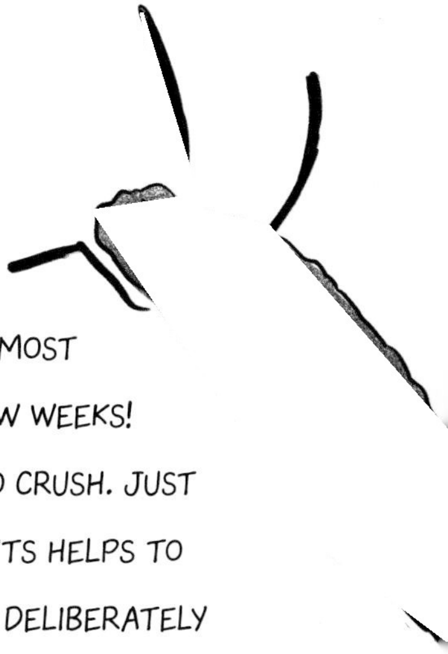

DIABOLICAL IRONCLAD BEETLE'S TOUGH EXOSKELETON

YOU'VE HEARD THE SAYING THAT CATS HAVE NINE LIVES? DIABOLICAL IRONCLAD BEETLES ONLY HAVE ONE LIFE, LIKE THE REST OF US, BUT THEY LIVE WAY LONGER THAN MOST BEETLES: SEVEN OR EIGHT YEARS, INSTEAD OF JUST A FEW WEEKS! PART OF THE REASON IS THAT THEY'RE REALLY TOUGH TO CRUSH. JUST AS BEETLE SAID, THE SHAPE OF HER EXOSKELETON'S JOINTS HELPS TO DISTRIBUTE PRESSURE. SCIENTISTS HAVE TESTED THIS BY DELIBERATELY RUNNING OVER IRONCLAD BEETLES WITH CARS. THE RESULTS: BEETLE 1, CAR 0. MOST BUGS CAN BE MOUNTED FOR DISPLAY BY PINNING THEM TO A BOARD. THE EXOSKELETON OF AN IRONCLAD BEETLE IS SO STRONG, COLLECTORS WHO WANT TO MOUNT THEM HAVE TO DRILL HOLES INTO THEIR BODIES!

READ MORE: SMITHSONIANMAG.COM/SMART-NEWS/SCIENTISTS-UNRAVEL-SECRETS-DIABOLICAL-IRONCLAD-BEETLES-NEAR-UNSQUISHABLE-STRENGTH-180976113

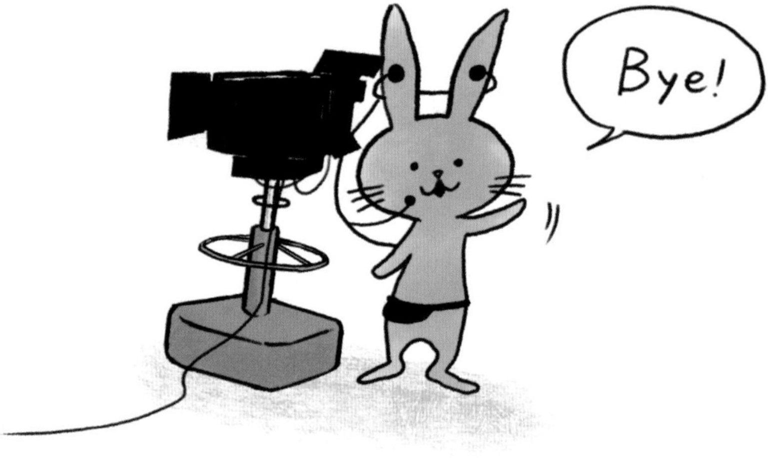
Bye!